CREDIT REPAIR SECRETS

LEARN THE STRATEGIES AND TECHNIQUES OF CONSULTANTS AND CREDIT ATTORNEYS TO FIX YOUR BAD DEBT AND IMPROVE YOUR BUSINESS OR PERSONAL FINANCE. INCLUDING DISPUTE LETTERS

DAVE ROBERT WARREN GRAHAM

©Copyright 2020 by Dave Robert Warren Graham

- All rights reserved –

ISBN: 9798595802147

The content contained within this book may not be reproduced, duplicated, or transmitted without direct written permission from the author or the publisher.

Under no circumstances will any blame or legal responsibility be held against the publisher, or author, for any damages, reparation, or monetary loss due to the information contained within this book. Either directly or indirectly.

Legal Notice:
This book is copyright protected. This book is only for personal use. You cannot amend, distribute, sell, use, quote, or paraphrase any part, or the content within this book, without the consent of the author or publisher.

Disclaimer Notice:
Please note the information contained within this document is for educational and entertainment purposes only. All effort has been executed to present accurate, up to date, and reliable, complete information. No warranties of any kind are declared or implied. Readers acknowledge that the author is not engaging in the rendering of legal, financial, medical or professional advice. The content within this book has been derived from various sources. Please consult a licensed professional before attempting any techniques outlined in this book.
By reading this document, the reader agrees that under no circumstances is the author responsible for any losses, direct or indirect, which are incurred as a result of the use of the information contained within this document, including, but not limited to, — errors, omissions, or inaccuracies

To my best friend Nans. Thanks to him for his valuable advice made me a successful entrepreneur and investor.

Dave R. W. Graham

Table of Contents

Introduction 1

CHAPTER 1: How to Get Started 7

CHAPTER 2: Understanding FCRA and Section 609 15

CHAPTER 3: How to Remove Hard Inquiries from Your Credit Report 23

CHAPTER 4: What the Credit Bureaus and the Lawyers Do Not Want You to Know 31

CHAPTER 5: Advice Nobody Tell You 35

CHAPTER 6: Your Financial Freedom 43

CHAPTER 7: Little Known Facts About Credit 51

CHAPTER 8: Effective Strategies for Repairing your Credit .. 57

CHAPTER 9: Controlling Various Kinds of Debt 65

CHAPTER 10: Guaranteed Methods to Protect Credit Score. 73

CHAPTER 11: The Credit Bureau 77

CHAPTER 12: How to Overcome Credit Card Debt 83

CHAPTER 13: Credit Repair from Scratch 91

Conclusion 97

BONUS:
Best Templates You Can Use to Work with Section 609 101

Let's Get Started.
Your File Organization Will Be Your Friend.

Introduction

Credit simply refers to the ability to borrow. We all need money to cater for various expenditures in life. However, just like any other economic resource, it is never enough, which means we are limited to what we can do since almost everything nowadays needs money. Where consumer price rises are quite apparent, it is getting tougher and tougher for the average person to afford a lifestyle. From consumer products to services, everything is now extremely expensive and people need to arrange for a bagful of money to lead a normal life. But it is not possible for them to arrange for this money through their monthly income alone and many have to rely on some external sources of credit. For instance, without additional or external financing, individuals and corporations cannot expand or grow financially.

They must have some money at their disposal to cater for all their monthly/ yearly financial needs. Borrowing is one of the most reliable sources of financing available, but, of course, it comes at a cost. If your credit hasn't improved very much, even though you're sure you've followed all the steps correctly, don't give up on trying to improve your credit. There're several things you can do, which will at least do some sort of damage control. The consequences of the negative items in your credit report will significantly be reduced. It is easy to get discouraged at this point and skip over the damage control step, but keep in mind that you have to put in some effort. The damage control might come in handy in the future, when you try again to repair your credit. All the information you've collected now will be useful in a future credit repair because some of the problems you've encountered now and that you found out are correct might be outdated (over seven years old) soon or your financial situation may improve over time, giving you more grounds for negotiation. Most importantly, by doing a bit of credit repairing and damage control now, this will give you a better starting point for a future credit repair that will be a lot more successful.

When you've reached this point, the first thing you must do is to make another list, with the problems you still have and give brief explanations to each. Letters containing no more than one hundred words each, explaining the reason for which you have that negative item on your credit report, will be attached to your credit report, so that when a creditor evaluates your application for a new credit, he will score it correctly and more in your favor. He now knows what's going on in your life and looks at more than just bad numbers. The letters will be part of your credit report permanently. Each short letter should say the same three things: something bad happened which caused you to default on your payments, but you have remedied that and bounced back and now you are up to date with everything. It should reflect how your financial behavior has improved. A damage control option might even be enough to get you a positive score on a credit application. Just make sure that, if your creditor is reviewing your report in an electronic format, they know that you have included one or more written statements. If he can't find the letters attached, you should have copies to send or hand them to the person working at the creditor's office that oversees your scores.

In this case, I recommend taking legal action. I know what you may be thinking. If you have financial problems, the cost of taking the issue to court will only add to these problems. You don't need a lawyer to take legal action for these issues. You can go to a small claims court with the proof you have gathered and do something about both the creditor and the credit reports agency. This will also entail some research, because the legal procedures involved are quite different from state to state. So, make sure that before you go to court you are prepared and brush up on the legislation in the part of the country you're in. If you have been wronged, it's worth the extra effort, especially since it will turn your credit from bad to good.

Negative Impacts of a Bad Credit Rating

A person with a bad credit score can still obtain credit but may feel the consequences are too much. A poor credit score will result in high-interest rates that can quickly become expensive, especially if you take longer to pay your accounts. A good, excellent, or exceptional credit score will reduce the interest charges and help you to save money in the long run. There are many other benefits to having a good credit score.

Your credit score is one way for the landlord to learn more about prospective tenants. The landlord or rental agency will often use your credit report to see if you pay on time or miss payments. Often, landlords are more willing to let property to people with a high credit score and will out rightly reject applicants with a low credit score. A good credit score is more likely to be approved for renting property since the landlord knows that the person is likely to pay.

Lenders will always choose a customer who has security when it comes to providing credit facilities. Owning an apartment, vehicle, or other assets will give banks the knowledge that you can pay them back. Stable assets help in negotiations with financial institutions for decreasing interest rates and down payments.

A person with a low credit score is perceived to be a high-risk client. The insurance company assumes that these people are more likely to claim insurance for unnecessary or fraudulent claims. This lack of trust results in higher insurance premiums.

A similar concept to the credit score is an insurance score used in some companies. The scores are not the same but the general principle of a higher score is better stays the same. Your credit score will greatly influence your insurance score.

Business credit cards offer similar rewards to personal credit cards. Still, you will only get these if the business has a good credit score. Most of the rewards for business will be in the form of a cash back percentage on the purchases made with the business credit card.

Why You Should Prioritize Credit Repair

It's simple. Credit is your credibility as related to your name and social security number. Your credibility is built from your financial borrowing patterns. You can develop creditability within any nation, organization, company, or individual, but being financially credible as we know it here in America comes from our dealings with lenders, banks and other forms of financial institutions. These financial entities furnish our information to credit agencies and companies that import and then summarized our activities into algorithms, which they use to generate credit scores. These credit agencies - also referred to as credit bureaus - are corporations that store our information in a file to identify our past and current creditability and determine our future credit worthiness. Your past behavior will dictate your current credit standing or whether you can be trusted to borrow a small sum, pay it back on set terms. If you can, you will then become more credible. It's that simple.

CHAPTER 1:

How to Get Started

Getting Started Cleaning up Your Credit, The Debt Snowball

Before you can start paying off your debt, it is important to come up with a plan for debt repayment. If you have just one debt to worry about, then the best strategy is to start repaying as much as you can every month. You must keep doing this until you are debt-free.

If you are like many others who are in debt, you might have multiple debts. You must try to develop the best repayment strategy that appeals to you and works well for your financial situation.

One method for repaying your debts is known as the debt snowball. You start repaying your debts in ascending order- starting from the smallest amount to the largest one. As you start clearing small loans, it will give you the motivation to keep going. You can start enjoying your small wins as you make your way to being debt-free.

You must start paying the minimum balance due on all your debts. Once you do this, divert all your extra funds toward the debt with the smallest amount. Once you clear this debt, all the money you spent on this repayment can be diverted towards the small debt on your list. Keep doing this until you paid off all your debts. Regardless of the rates of interest payable, you must start with the smallest sum due and make your way to the largest one. If you ever played in the snow and made a snowball, you will realize that it keeps collecting more and more snow as the snowball rolls on the ground and becomes bigger. So, every small debt you repay will free up sufficient funds to repay the debt.

Let us assume that you have four debts, and their details are as follows:

- An auto loan repayable at 4.5% for $16,000.
- A student loan repayable at 6.5% for $30,000.
- A personal loan repayable at 8% for $10,000.
- A credit card debt repayable at 21% for $7000.

So, you will start by repaying your credit card debt, which is at $7000. Once you repay this diet and have paid the minimum balance due for all the other loans. All the interest that was payable towards the credit card debt can be successfully redirected toward the other loans' payment. You will start with your credit card debt, then the personal loan, auto loan, and then finally the student loan.

This is a great technique to pay your debts, especially if you have several small debts. At times, it can be rather overwhelming and scary when you look at a major debt. It can also be the reason for losing your motivation.

To avoid this, when you start clearing the small debts, the number of loans you have to repay will reduce. If you have five loans, and you repay two loans, the figure somehow looks more manageable. Instead of worrying about repaying all the five loans simultaneously, you can concentrate on repaying the smallest ones, and then be left with only the major debts.

How debt snowball method works:

Step 1: List the debts from lowest to highest.

Stage 2: Make minimum payments on all but the smallest debts

Stage 3: Follow this process with as you clear all your debt. The more you pay off, the more your freed-up money grows like a snowball going downhill.

What You Should Include in Your Debt Snowball?

Your debt snowball should include all non-mortgage debt, a loan that is described as anything else you owe to anyone.

- Car notes
- Credit card balances
- Home equity loans
- Medical bills
- Payday loans
- Personal loans
- Student loans

When compared to the Avalanche method, you might end up paying more interest in the long run by using the snowball method. Since the interest rates are never considered in this method, any account, which has a higher rate of interest and a large outstanding balance, will be left towards the end. So, the interest payable will increase.

Is Credit Repair Ethical?

Beware, not all credit repair companies are ethical. Do not fall for scams that promise they can take a bad credit record and turn it around overnight. Or that guarantee they can "force" the credit bureaus to remove all negative (but accurate) information from your credit file immediately. It takes time and your cooperation to improve your credit. Trust me when I tell you that a credit repair company cannot push around the large credit bureaus. Never mind order them to do things like immediately remove foreclosures or missed payments from their client's records. Inaccurate information can be easily fixed. However, removing accurate negative information takes a plan and is rarely done overnight. That usually requires filing official disputes, and careful negotiations with your creditors.

Some credit repair companies not only misrepresent what they can do for you, but also practice illegal or fraudulent ways of trying to improve your credit. They will often reorganize as a non-profit to get around state and federal laws that govern the industry. If you are desperate enough, you may be tempted to risk some of these illegal actions, but we would not recommend it. Also, be wary of credit repair companies that want to be paid up front. People have lost hundreds, and in some cases thousands of dollars to credit repair scams.

The Warning Signs When Choosing a Credit Repair Company
- -They recommend that you do not contact credit bureaus directly.
- -They do not disclose your legal rights or what you can do yourself.
- -They want you to pay upfront based on their verbal promises before they do any work. It is illegal for them to charge you up front. They can only charge you after they have completed the services they contracted for.
- -They suggest unethical or illegal actions such as making false statements on a loan application, misrepresenting your social security number, or obtaining an EIN under false pretenses. The use of these tactics could constitute general fraud, civil fraud, mail fraud, wire fraud, and get you into a lot of trouble.

Once you receive a copy of your free credit report, take note of your three-digit credit score, and note any damage to your credit standing due to an increased credit utilization, derogatory marks on your report, missed/late payments on your credit cards, closure of old accounts or recent applications for a new credit card/loan. Sometimes, credit repair can be very simple when it involves fixing disputing mistakes shown on your credit reports with the credit reporting agencies/providers, or an extensive repair, when the issue is about identity theft or fundamental financial issues like budgeting. While you seek to rebuild and repair your credit, you rectify a poor credit score or pay a company to report and remove any incorrect items from your report. Your credit history is vital to understanding your credit standing. You can file disputes where you observe inaccurate information on your credit report.

What is Credit Repair?

Remember, credit repair entails actions taken to rectify inaccuracies in your credit reports, and (re)build an awesome credit history for an improved/higher credit score. The Fair Credit Reporting Act (FCRA) stipulates consumers' accurate information on the credit bureau's files, and it approves consumers' right to dispute questionable information. A poor credit is a credit score below 580, and any credit sore between 580-669 is rated fairly by lenders, even though it is questionable for loan approvals. Suppose your credit score falls in these ranges, due to late student loan payment, collection accounts, foreclosure, or years of increased credit card balance. In that case, this will drag your credit score down significantly which will make you unqualified for the approval of a new credit card or loan. Surprisingly, you could take matters into your own hands and repair your credit yourself with a copy of your credit report.

Self-Credit Repair Step

Credit repair is not only about disputing inaccuracies in your report, but it is also about concentrating your present actions in the management of your credit for a positive credit score. To this effect, you should adhere to the following instructions:

1. Know your credit standing by checking your credit report;
2. Be current on your monthly bills;
3. Dispute any error to correct your credit report for a better credit;
4. Know your current credit utilization rate;
5. Create payment reminders;
6. Choose credit responsibly;
7. Spend less based on your purchase by creating a limit;
8. Improve and think about your credit history;
9. Be current about the number of your credit accounts;
10. Ensure you pay your credit card balances;
11. Avoid applications of new loan.

The Truth About CPNs, or Credit Privacy Numbers

So much hype is built up around the magical theory of CPN numbers. Some people referred to them as Credit Profile Numbers, or Credit Privacy Numbers. I have even heard people say Celebrity Privacy Numbers. From my understanding CPN numbers aren't anything new and have been around for a long time. The concept is simple, you can use your same name, alter your birthdate by one year and one day, or keep the same birthday. Still, you must find a new address that has never been associated with your social security number. Ideally, a CPN address should be from a zip code that your social security number has never been associated with. Once you take this information and apply for a credit line with a major creditor, this will tri-merge your new number and have a brand-new credit file with all 3 major credit bureaus.

Having a CPN number serves best the people who have messed up credit and just want a fresh start because they may not know how or don't want to learn how to fix their credit. Law Enforcement has been known to incorporate this tactic to create new identities for those within the constraints of protective custody, or even deep-cover federal agents. For the everyday person, a new number and a new credit file is looked at as a shortcut, most are just too lazy to get started on fixing their credit as it is easier to start from scratch rather than repairing their credit. Others may want to utilize multiple identities to carry more debt, defraud creditors or shield themselves from the liability of everyday life.

CHAPTER 2:

Understanding FCRA and Section 609

A Summary of Your Rights Under the Fair Credit Reporting Act: What Is the Purpose of the Fair Credit Reporting Act? How Does the FCRA Help Consumers?

When you are going about trying to fix your credit, it can often feel as though the deck is stacked against you, however, the truth of the matter is that several laws can help you to even the odds when it comes to dealing with both creditors and credit bureaus.

FCRA: The FCRA does more than just provide you with a free credit report each year. It also regulates the various credit reporting organizations. It ensures that the information they gather on you is both accurate and fair. This means that if you see inaccurate information on your credit report, and report it to the relevant agency, they are legally required to look into the matter and resolve it, typically within 30 days. The same applies to agencies or organizations that generally add details to your credit report. Finally, suppose an organization that reviews your credit report decides to charge your more or declines to do business with you based on what they find in your report. In that case, they are legally obligated to let you know why and what report they found the negative information in.

While this won't help you with that lender, if the information is inaccurate, you will know where to go to clear up the issue. Additionally, if you report an inaccuracy and the credit reporting agency ignores your request you can sue them to recover the damages or a minimum of $2,500. You may also be able to win an additional amount based on punitive damages and legal fees and any other associated costs. You must file legal proceedings within 5 years of when this occurs.

What Is Section 609? Is a 609 Dispute Letter Effective?

The first thing that we need to take a look at here when it comes to our credit scores is what Section 609 is all about. This is going to be one of the best ways for you to get your credit score up, and outside of a little calling or sending out mail, you will not have to do as much to get it all done. Let's dive in now and see if we can learn a bit more about it.

The FCRA or the Fair Credit Reporting Act will cover a lot of the aspects and the components of credit checking to make sure that it can maintain a reasonable amount of privacy and accuracy along the way. This agency will list out all the responsibilities that credit reporting companies, and any credit bureaus, will have, and it also includes the rights of the consumer, which will be your rights in this situation. This Act is going to be the part that will govern how everything is going to work to ensure that all parties are treated fairly.

Other issues that are addressed in this act will be done in a manner that is the most favorable to the consumer. This Act is going to limit the access that third-parties can have to your file. You have to provide your consent before someone can go through and look at your credit score, whether it is a potential employer or another institution providing you with funding.

They are not able to get in and just look at it. Keep in mind that if you do not agree for them to take a look at the information, it is going to likely result in you not getting the funding that you want, because there are very few ways that the institution can fairly assess the risk that you pose to them in terms of creditworthiness.

There are several ways that a credit agency can go through and break or violate the FCRA, so this allows the consumer a way to protect themselves if that proves to be something that needs to happen.

Another thing to note about all of this is that the FCRA will be divided into sections. And each of these sections will come with a unique set of rules that all credit bureaus need to follow. In particular, Section 609 of the FCRA will deal with disclosure and is going to put all the burdens of providing the right kind of documentation on the credit bureaus.

This may sound a little bit confusing, but it means that you may have debt or another negative item that is on your credit report. Still, there is a way to get around this without having to wait for years to get that to drop off your report or having to pay back a debt that you are not able to afford.

Keep in mind that this is not meant to be a method for you to take on many debts that you can't afford and then just dump them. But on occasion, there could be a few that you can fight and get an instant boost to your credit score in the process.

You do not have to come up with a way of proving if the item on the credit report is legitimate or not. Instead, that is up to the credit bureaus. And there are many cases where they are not able to do this. Whether they bought the debt and did not have the proper documentation, or there is something else that is wrong with it, the credit company may not prove that you are the owner of it or that you owe on it at all. If this is the case, they have to remove the information from your credit report. When a bad debt is taken off, or even a collection is taken off, that does nothing but a lot of good for your overall score.

Some of Your Rights Under Section 609 and How You Can Use These to Your Advantage. How to Correctly Dispute Errors on Your Credit Report.

According to Section 609 of the Fair Credit Reporting Act, the credit bureaus cannot list any credit agreements without verifying their validity first. The creditor is supposed to send a copy of the bureaus' credit agreement to validate and keep in case there are any inquiries.

This is important because the bureaus generally skip this step. It is expensive and time consuming for them to verify all the information they receive. By law, the bureaus are required to provide proof that they have verified the information within thirty days. Suppose they cannot prove the original agreement or subsequent evidence of negative listings, and you can prove your identity. In that case, they must remove the listing. It does not matter if the information is accurate or not. That is why it's important to monitor your credit.

To take advantage of this law, the first thing you need to do is to send a physical letter to the billing inquiries address that the creditor provides. If they turn down your request, you can ask for all the documentation saying why they turned you down.

A subset of this law is known as the Hidden Gem Law, this means you can dispute any transaction made within 100 miles of your home, or anywhere in your home state, which exceeds $50. As long as you make a good faith effort to dispute the transaction and return the item or stop using the service, the company will likely refund it.

If the debt collector breaks these rules or acts in other ways they are not allowed then you can file a private lawsuit and be recouped costs, fees and damages. What's more, you don't even need to prove damages and you will likely be awarded a minimum of $1,000.

Ways to Approach the Financial Institution

If the credit reporting agency is struggling to alter your report and think the information is incomplete or wrong --you will want to take action. Below are a few suggestions that will assist you with your attempts.

Contact the Creditor Directly

Contacts the lender, which supplied the advice and demand it inform the credit. Request to Creditor composes your letter or to Eliminate. You can use inaccurate Information. You receive a letter from the lender and should be deleted from the credit history if you send a copy of the letter to the bureau that made the faulty report. If you contacted the Funding, it does not need to manage this dispute unless you supply it. Since you also demonstrate a foundation for the belief, and the dispute wasn't properly researched should you increase your complaint, just like the president or CEO, the provider is very likely to reply. If the company cannot help you remove the inaccurate info, call the credit reporting agency.

Document another Dispute with the Credit Reporting Agency with More Information

If you have info backs up your claim, it is possible to submit a fresh dispute. Make sure to provide info. Should you dispute the mistake without giving any info to the bureau, it will determine that your dispute is frivolous, so the bureau does not need to inquire into the issue.

File a Complaint about the Credit Reporting Agency

You can file a complaint regarding a Credit reporting bureau together with the Consumer Financial Protection Bureau (CFPB). The CFPB attempt to have a response and will forward your complaint. Suppose the CFPB believes another government agency will be able to assist you. In that case, it allows you to know and forward your complaint.

File a Complaint Concerning the Creditor

Suppose the lender supplied The erroneous or incomplete data fails to revise it or notify the credit reporting service of a correction (or even if it advises the credit reporting bureau of this alteration, but reports the incorrect information again after). In that case, you might file a complaint with the Federal Trade Commission (FTC). Or, if the lender is a big institution, you might file a complaint. The CFPB manages Types of agencies, and that means a complaint can document. If you are unsure which agency to contact, begin with CFPB or even the FTC, which will forward your complaint. Normally, you won't be represented by these government agencies. However, they could send an inquiry, and they may take action when there are complaints or proof of wrongdoing.

Complain for Your State Consumer Protection Agency

Some countries have to credit reporting lenders or bureaus furnishing information. File a complaint with the attorney general or consumer protection bureau of your state.

Consider Adding an Explanatory Statement for Your Credit Report

You've got the right Statement to your credit score. As soon as you submit a statement regarding the dispute using a credit reporting agency, the agency must include your statement--or a list of it. It might limit your announcement. In case the agency helps you in writing the excuse. There is not a term limit. Nonetheless, it is a fantastic idea to maintain the announcement shortly. In this way, the credit reporting agency is inclined to utilize your remark.

CHAPTER 3:

How to Remove Hard Inquiries from Your Credit Report

What Is a Hard Inquiry? Should You Remove Hard Inquiries?

All hard inquiries show up on your credit report. They account for about 10% of your total credit score according to the FICO model. If you pull up your credit report, it is a soft inquiry. If any lender or a creditor checks your credit report to pre-approve you for any existing, of course, it is also soft inquiry. All soft inquiries are exempt from your credit report, and it won't influence your credit score.

Your credit report and credit score will be checked by a potential lender whenever you apply for a loan, credit card, or other similar credit. However, the lender will do so only after obtaining your approval for the same. Once the lender has your approval, he can approach the credit bureau and request your credit report. Since this inquiry is primarily made to ensure your creditworthiness, it will show up in the credit report.

Now, let us look at why hard inquiries matter and the way they affect your credit report. Suppose your credit report is riddled with multiple hard inquiries made within a short period. In that case, it is a red flag for all potential lenders. Multiple hard inquiries show that you are trying to open multiple new accounts. This, in turn, implies that you are in dire need of funds and that your financial position is shaky. It might also be a sign of poor budgeting and the inability to manage your finances. So, it paints a rather negative image in the minds of potential lenders or creditors.

At times, people make multiple inquiries because they are shopping for the best deal available in the market. Credit rating models are reasonable, and they do consider this possibility. For instance, if you're looking for a mortgage and have made several hard inquiries within 30 days, then all this will be treated as a single hard inquiry. Multiple inquiries will be pardoned provided they are all related to a specific type of credit and are made within a short period. Usually, you will not be denied loans because of the number of hard inquiries on your credit report. A hard inquiry is one of the many factors taken into consideration while determining your creditworthiness. Such inquiries tend to appear on your report for two years. As time passes by, their effect on your credit score reduces. You won't be disqualified for credit by a lender merely because of the hard inquiries. After all, it accounts for only 10% of your total credit score.

If you notice that a hard inquiry on your report is inaccurate, you can raise a dispute about the same and get it removed. If a specific hard inquiry was made without your permission, then it is erroneous. If you notice any hard inquiries made by any unfamiliar lenders in your credit report, please look into it. It can be a sign of identity theft. Carefully go through your credit report and check the accuracy of all the entries reported on it. If any inaccurate hard inquiries are removed from your report, it can help improve your credit score.

Suppose a hard inquiry was made without your authorization or prior approval. In that case, you can get it removed from your credit report along with your credit history. You can do this only when you had no prior knowledge about the hard inquiries. You can also get any other inquiries removed from the credit report, which were made because you were pressurized into accepting an application process even when you weren't interested. Here are a couple of hard inquiries that can be easily disputed and removed from your credit report.

- Any such inquiries that were made without your authorization or consent.
- Any inquiries made without your prior knowledge.
- Any inquiry wherein you were pressurized to accept such an inquiry.
- When the number of inquiries present on the credit report exceed the ones you made.

If you notice any inaccurate hard inquiries on the credit report, send a letter contacting the appropriate credit bureau for its removal. Send the same letter to the concerned lender as well. Only use certified mail for sending both these letters. A certified mail will keep a record of the delivery and the receipt of the concerned letter. You can hold onto this record as legal proof, and it will come in handy if the receiver denies the letter's acceptance.

Before you send a notice for the removal of a credit inquiry, you must notify the lender. Before you take any legal action, you must notify the concerned parties. At times, the lender might not be as responsive to your request as the credit bureau. I suggest that you don't give up and get any wrong entries removed from your credit report at the earliest. While sending a letter to remove the discrepancy, don't forget to attach a copy of your credit report along with it.

Suppose you make multiple hard inquiries within a short period. In that case, it is usually considered to be an indication of filing for bankruptcy. It shows that you are running out of funds or have already exhausted the resources available. Apart from this, it makes your financial position seem highly unstable and makes you look like a flight risk for all potential creditors. If you look into multiple sources of credit at the same time for various reasons, it indicates bankruptcy. So, start being mindful of all the hard inquiries you make.

Disputing Inaccurate Hard Inquiries Yourself

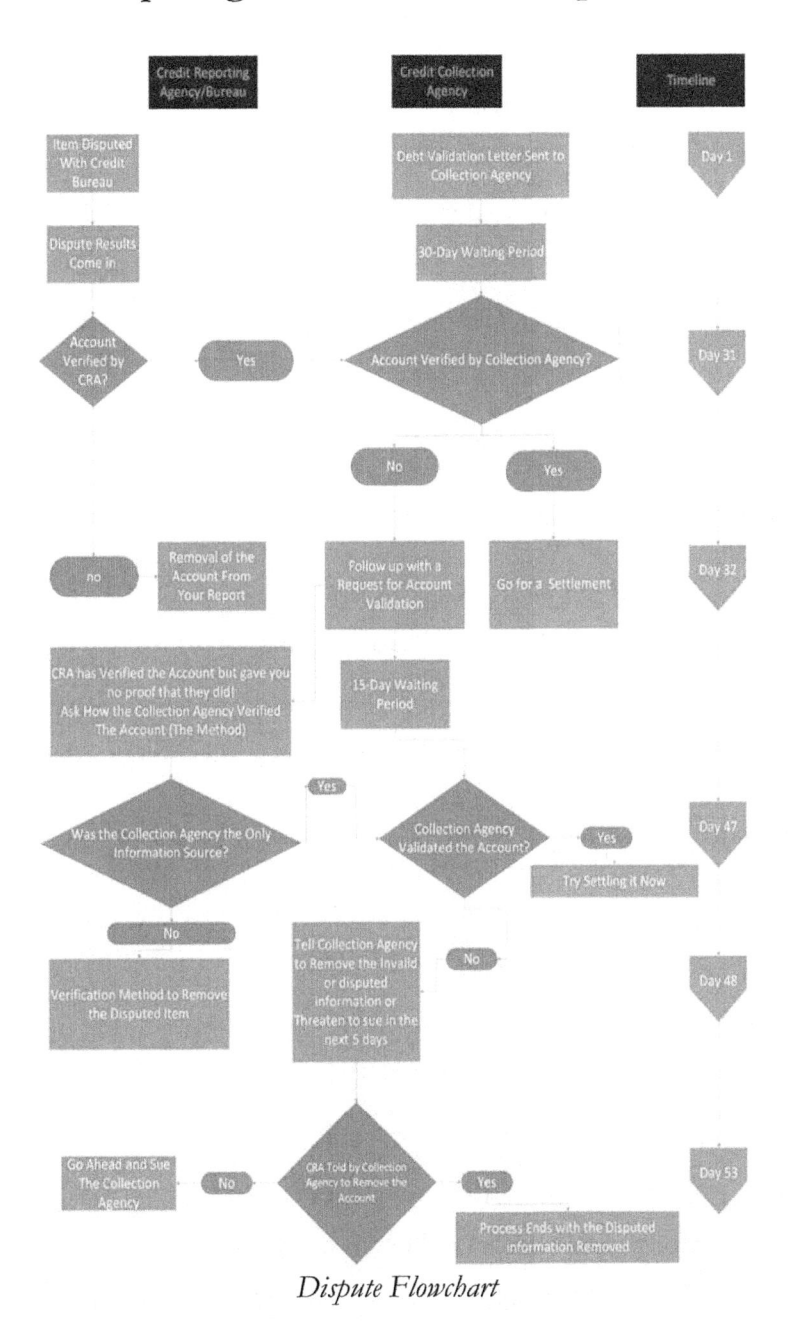

Dispute Flowchart

The FCRA's regulations state that both the credit bureau (credit reporting company) and the information provider are responsible to correct inaccuracies and fill out incomplete information correctly in your credit report. The information provider is the person, company or organization that provides information about you to the credit reporting company, and may include banks, healthcare providers, grocery stores, clothes shops, landlords, etc.

You have certain rights under FCRA as well.

These include:

- The right to receive a copy of your credit report. This copy should include all updated information from your file at the time of your request.
- A company that denied your credit request must inform you of the name and address of the credit reporting agency that they contacted. This is only when the company denied the application based on the information that the credit reporting company provided.
- Suppose you are unsure of the completeness and accuracy of the information in your credit report and you want to challenge it. In that case, you should file a dispute with the credit bureau and the company that gave them the information. Both credit bureau and the information provider are bound by law to investigate the dispute you file.

- If someone received your credit report in the last year for most reasons, or in the last two years for employment reasons, you have every right to know their name.
- You have every right to add a summary explanation if you're not satisfied with the resolution of your dispute.

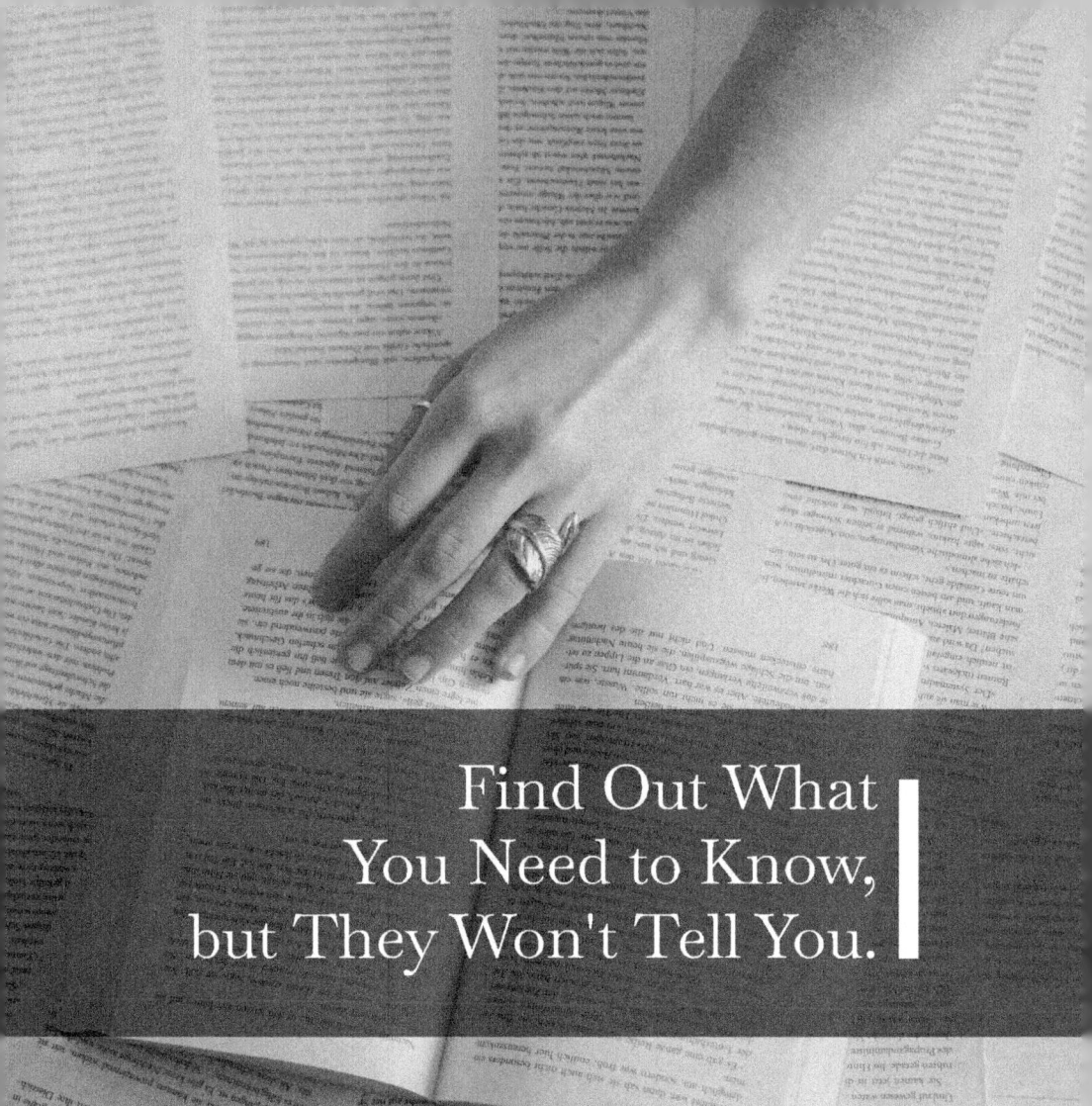

Find Out What You Need to Know, but They Won't Tell You.

CHAPTER 4:

What the Credit Bureaus and the Lawyers Do Not Want You to Know

How to Deal with the Big Three Credit Bureaus. Who Are, How to Work

In the United States, there are three major credit bureaus: Trans Union, Experian and Equifax. Each of these companies is responsible for collecting information about all consumers' personal information, habits for paying bills and other financial data to form credit reports. Therefore, your credit report is unique to you because your spending habits, credit cards, loans, and more will differ from other consumers. Furthermore, each credit reporting agency will have a unique formula for calculating your credit score. The information will be similar, but there can be some slight differences.

Credit bureaus are privately held, billion-dollar organizations whose primary reason for existing is to make cash; that is what revenue driven organizations do right? They keep data that lenders furnish them - whether accurate or inaccurate - about our credit association with them and sell it.

Basic, right? This straightforward plan of action generates over $4 Billion per year!

One wellspring of income for them originates from selling the information on our credit reports to different lenders, managers, insurance agencies, credit card organizations - and whoever else you approve to see your credit information. In addition to the fact that they provide them with crude data; yet they likewise sell them various methods for examining the data to decide the risk of stretching out credit to us. In addition to trading our information to lenders, they likewise sell our information to us - credit scores, credit observing administrations, extortion security, wholesale fraud prevention - interestingly enough this region has quickly gotten perhaps the greatest wellspring of income. Furthermore, those pre-endorsed offers in our letter drop each week; or garbage mail? That's right; they got our information from the credit bureaus as well. Organizations buy in to an assistance provided by the three credit bureaus that sell them a rundown of consumer's credit information that fit a pre-decided criterion.

Today, credit bureaus consistently accumulate information from creditors (banks; credit-card guarantors; mortgage organizations, which have practical experience in loaning cash to home buyers; and different businesses that stretch out credit to people and businesses) and amass it into files on singular consumers and businesses, while refreshing their current files. Information usually remains on a credit report for seven years before being evacuated.

Every one of these three organizations assembles and appropriates information separately. Credit scores and reports vary somewhat from bureau to bureau. Each organization keeps up around 200 million singular consumer credit files. Frequently, a lender will utilize an average of the three unique bureaus' credit evaluations when choosing whether or not to make a loan.

Credit bureaus collect information from various sources by consumer information. The activity is done for various reasons and includes data from singular consumers. Included is the information concerning a people charge payments and their getting. Utilized for evaluating creditworthiness, the information provides lenders with an outline of your accounts if a loan repayment is required. The interest rates charged on a loan are additionally worked out concerning the kind of credit score shown by your experience. Like this, it is not a uniform procedure, and your credit report is the significant instrument that affects future loans.

Based on risk based valuing, it pegs various risks on the various customers to decide the cost you will acquire as a borrower. Done as credit rating, it is an assistance provided to various interested parties in the public. Terrible credit histories are affected for the most part by settled court commitments which mark you for high interest rates every year. For example, duty liens and bankruptcies shut you out of the conventional credit lines. They may require a great deal of arrangement for any loan to be offered by the bank.

Bureaus collect and examine credit information including financial data, personal information, and elective data. Various sources give this generally marked data furnishers. These have an exceptional association with the credit bureaus. An average gathering of data furnishers would comprise creditors, lenders, utilities, and debt collection agencies. Pretty much any association which has had payment involvement in the consumer is qualified including courts. Any data collected for this situation is provided to the credit bureaus for grouping. When it is accumulated, the data is placed into specific repositories and files claimed by the bureau. The information is made accessible to customers upon request. The idea of such information is important to lenders and managers.

The information is material in various conditions; credit evaluation and business thought are simply part of these. The consumer may likewise require the information to check their score. The home proprietor may need to check their inhabitants' report before renting an apartment. Since borrowers saturate the market, the scores will, in general, be robotic. Straightforward examination would deal with this by giving the client a calculation for speedy appraisal. Checking your score once every other year should deal with errors in your report.

Individuals from the public are qualified for one free credit report from every one of the significant bureaus. This is organized in the Fair Credit Report Act, FCTA. Other government rules associated with the consumer's assurance incorporate Fair and Accurate Credit Transaction Act, Fair Credit Billing Act and Regulation B. Statutory bodies have also been made for the regulation of the credit bureaus. The Fair-Trade Commission serves to as a controller for the consumer credit report agencies. Simultaneously, the Office of the Comptroller of Currency fills in as a manager of all banks going about as furnishers.

CHAPTER 5:

Advice Nobody Tell You

Advice on Right Mind-set for Credit Management

Many folks suffer a financial crisis at some point. They may have to deal with overspending, losing a job, a family member or personal illness. These financial problems can be and usually are, overwhelming. To make these situations worse, most people don't even know where to solve these financial dilemmas. Our goal here is to shine some light on the strategies to help get youth Accumulating basic consumer debt will chain you into slavery and you could spend your life held down by your obligations to repay these loans.

What type of credit should you get? That depends on what you plan to do with the money. The most used types of credit are secured and signature credits. For smaller loans, there's no need for that, as no institution would like to end up with a store of household items, so they lend you money or issue a credit card in your name simply based on the strength of your credit so far.

DAVE ROBERT WARREN GRAHAM

There is hope; you as the borrower have many options to get rid of debt. You can take advantage of budgeting and other techniques, such as debt consolidation, debt settlement, credit counselling and bankruptcy procedures. You just have to choose the best strategy that will work for you. When choosing from the various options, you have to consider your debt level, discipline, and plans.

Advice on How to Manage Bankruptcy and How it Will Affect Credit

Whether you struggle with debt, are unable to meet all your payments on time, have missed multiple payments on your mortgage or car loan, have maxed out your credit cards, are balancing payments on several credit cards to try to keep up to date, or are slipping back on a lot of unsecured debt, the effective bankruptcy option may be what you need to offset your income and debt. If you think the worst possible thing for your credit is bankruptcy, think again. Suppose you're already behind on payments and keep falling further behind or have accounts in collection. In that case, bankruptcy may help you start building a strong credit history sooner rather than later.

Before considering how bankruptcy will work for you, you must first familiarize yourself with the various types of bankruptcy, grasp what bankruptcy can and cannot do, and know how it will affect your reputation.

Bankruptcy is a powerful tool for removing or rising most unsecured debts. It can even cut down on most secured debts— giving you a fresh start. But it will live up to 10 years on your credit report (longer if you apply for a $150,000 or more loan), which is longer than almost any other derogatory thing in your history.

Even though a bankruptcy will lower your credit score immediately, the impact may be smaller than you think. "Someone who had spotless credit and a very good FICO score might expect a huge decrease in their ratings, according to Fair Isaac. On the other hand, someone with more derogatory things already reported at their credit report could only see a small decrease in their ratings. "Fair Isaac also warns that the greater the effect on your ranking, the more accounts included in the bankruptcy filing.

Ironically, a bankruptcy will help you start building good credit faster than if you don't file for bankruptcy and keep struggling with more debt than you can afford, particularly if you end up filing bankruptcy again later. Eliminating or eliminating loans by bankruptcy would help you (when the bankruptcy is over) accomplish the two most important goals for a good credit score: meeting your payments on time (35% of your FICO score) and not using the bulk of your available credit (30% of your FICO score). Creditors differ in how they can offer credit or good interest rates and repayment conditions shortly after a bankruptcy. Still, they tend to treat the most recent credit issues as more relevant than older problems.

Check Your Credit Report Regularly

When you monitor your credit, you will be able to tell when your report changes. Things to keep an eye on could include your payment history and account balance changes, among other things.

There are many apps and sites like Credit Sesame and Credit Karma which help you monitor credit for free and inform you anytime there is a change, to ensure you know what is going on with your credit.

There are tons of tricks and tips you can utilize in maintaining and even improving your credit score. A few of the top steps you can take include not overspending, making payments on time, and paying consistently. All of these will ensure you don't reduce the credit score you battled so hard to build.

How to Negotiate and Settle Large Debt

Knowing which revolving debts to pay off first matters. I will cover 2 different approaches. Which you choose will depend on your need and how well you know yourself.

The first approach I call the Snow Ball method. This is the approach I use personally because I know I need to see results quickly or lose interest.

Here's how it works…

Any extra income you have is used to pay down this balance first. Once the card is paid off, take that same money you were using to pay the first card off and pay down the second card. This works because you have larger and larger sums of money to knock your debt down.

From a psychological point of view, it's very rewarding to see cards with zero balances accumulating and having larger and larger sums of money to drive your next balance down. While extremely effective, the Snow Ball method is not the best method for improving your FICO scores.

Most people assume that paying down the card with the highest interest rate would be the next logical step, but that's incorrect. You need to think like FICO and understand what FICO considers important.

When calculating your credit scores, FICO takes four criteria into consideration:

- Overall combined utilization
- Line item utilization
- Number of accounts with a balance
- Number of highly utilized credit cards

Utilization just means how much of your credit you're using. Take out your spread sheet again. First, you'll want to pay off any cards that have low balances on them. Remember that using too many cards is not a good thing, so always keep at least one card at zero.

Next, you'll list your lenders in order of highest utilization to lowest.

For example:

Your Pay-off Priority List should look like this:

- Citibank
- US Bank
- Macy's
- Shell
- Sears

Citibank is first because the amount owed is small... and having a credit card account with a zero balance will increase your score. The other revolving credit cards' order was based on the utilization percentage of each card. This is how you hack FICO's scoring formula to optimize your credit scores.

You will start to see a credit score increase in about 30-40 days. Lenders only update their records with the credit bureaus once a month. The date they update is normally about 10 days after your due date. It's important to note that using your credit cards while you're paying them down is counterproductive.

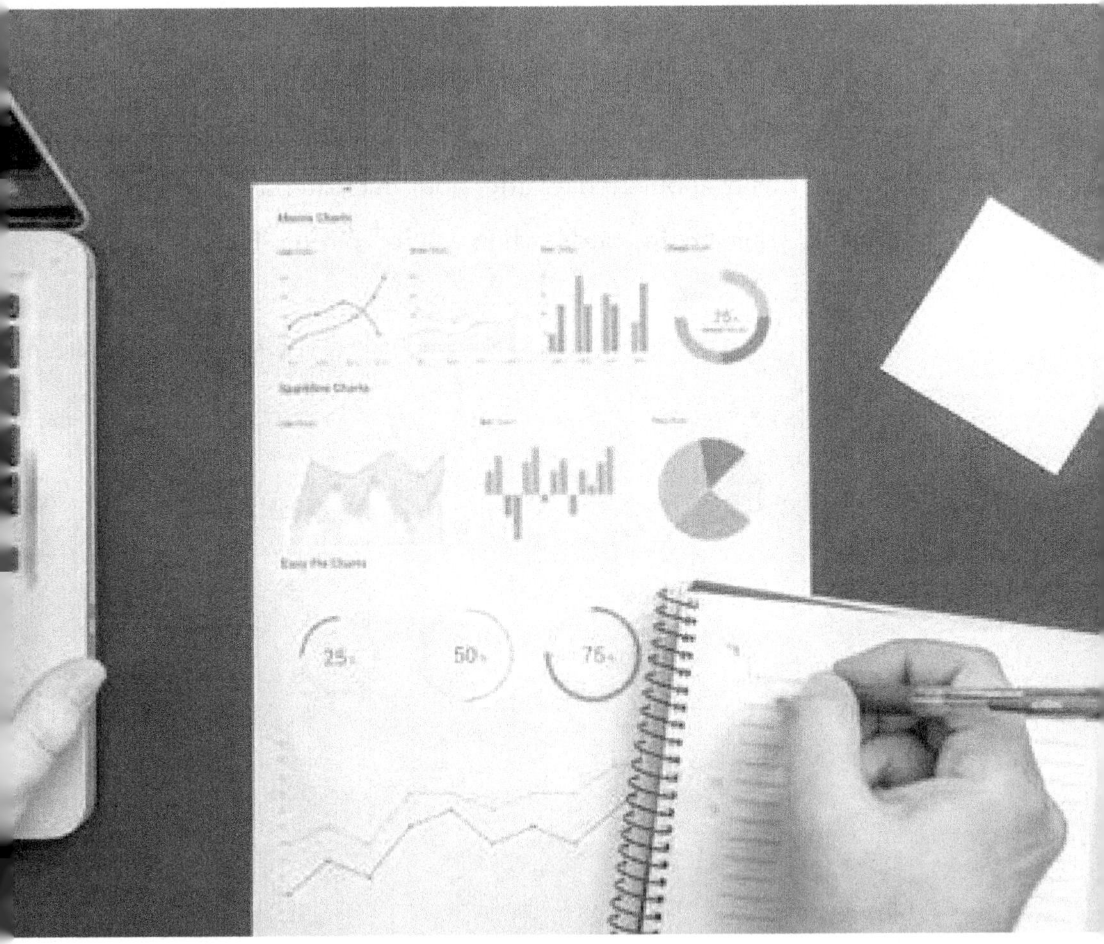

CHAPTER 6:

Your Financial Freedom

Financial freedom is a concept that people love to think about but rarely feel like they can reach.

What Is Meant by Financial Freedom?

Financial freedom has no set definition. However, it typically means that you are living comfortably and saving for retirement and in general. It can also mean that you have an emergency reserve set up. In general, financial freedom can mean whatever you want it to mean for you. For example, a prior college student may not think that financial freedom includes paying off all their student loans. This is because, at least currently, a college student who needs to pay their own way realizes they will always be paying off their student loans. However, they might feel that student loans are the only debt they should have. Therefore, being able to pay off credit cards or medical bills leads them to financial freedom.

Some people might feel that financial freedom indicates they have absolutely no debt or loans. This includes them having paid off their mortgage and any car loans. They might also feel that to reach financial freedom, they need to be investing in a CD, bond, or even in the stock market.

Other people may feel that financial freedom means they are no longer tied down to a job. They can live off their savings or a passive income, and they can retire and enjoy life through traveling.

Credit Cards and Financial Freedom - Is It Safe?

One of the biggest questions people have regarding financial freedom is whether they can have any credit card accounts in their name. While you may not owe anything on your credit cards (in fact, you might only owe one you pay off in full every month), is this still financial freedom? In general, this is completely determined by your definition of financial freedom. However, if you ever find yourself not being able to pay off your credit card every month, this is not financial freedom. In most cases, financial freedom does mean you no longer have any debt, or at least that you are free from unnecessary debt, such as credit cards.

Most people are quick to state that financial freedom and credit cards do not go together simply because they are not safe with each other. This is because it is often easy to fall back into thinking you can pay the amount off everything each month and become unable to do so. In general, people who reach financial freedom feel that credit cards allow for more of a trap and keep them from reaching financial freedom.

However, other people who feel they have reached financial freedom state that as long as you can manage your credit cards wisely, they can be included with your freedom. Some of them also advise that you set up a financial freedom plan. Within this plan, you will state your conditions of using a credit card. Of course, you need to be self-disciplined enough to follow your condition.

The Best Habits to Help You Reach and Protect Your Financial Freedom

When it comes to financial freedom, there are dozens of habits and tips that people provide to help you reach your financial freedom. It is important to note that because financial freedom can vary depending on the person's definition, some tips and habits might work for you while others may not. You need to find the ones that work best for you, not the ones that other people say are the best. Therefore, I will give you a fairly large list as I want you to make sure that you can find some of the best habits and tips so you can reach financial freedom and protect it.

1. **Make a Budget**

Making and keeping a budget is one of the first steps everyone should take while heading towards your financial freedom. Even though you might find yourself changing your budget now and then, as you will add or delete bills or receive a different income, you always want to follow it. Not only will this help you in reaching your financial freedom, but continuing to follow your budget will also protect your financial freedom.

Furthermore, creating a monthly budget can ensure that all your bills are being paid and you know exactly where your money is going. For example, you will be able to see how much money you spend on groceries, gas, and eating out at restaurants. This will help you know where you can decrease your spending, which will allow you to save more. There are a lot of great benefits when it comes to creating and sticking with a household budget.

2. Set Up Automatic Savings Account

If you work for an organization that automatically places a certain percentage of your check into a savings account, take advantage of this. It gives you the idea that you never had the money to begin with, which means you don't plan for it. You won't find yourself taking the money out of savings unless you need it for an emergency. Furthermore, you can set up a separate savings account where this money will go. You can make it so you rarely see this account, however, you want to make sure that your money is deposited and everything looks right on your account. But, the point of this account if you do not touch it, even if you have an emergency. Instead, you will set up a different account for emergency basis.

The other idea to this is you pay yourself first. This is often something that people don't think about because they are more worried about paying off their debt. However, many financial advisors say that you are always number one when it comes to your finances. While you want to pay your bills, you also need to make sure that you and your family are taken care of.

3. Keep Your Credit in Mind Without Obsessing Over It

Your credit score is important, but it is not the most important thing in the world. People often fall into the trap of becoming obsessed over their credit score, especially when trying to improve it. One factor to remember is that your credit score is typically only updated every so often. Therefore, you can decide to set time aside every quarter to check on your credit report. When you do this, you not only want to check your score, but you also want to check what the credit bureaus are reporting. Just like you want to make sure everything is correct on your bank account, you want to do the same thing for your credit report.

4. It Is Fine to Live Below Your Means

One of the biggest factors of financial freedom and maintaining it is you can make your bills and comfortably live throughout the month. To do this, you need to make sure that the money coming into your home is more than the money going out. In other words, you want to live below your means.

This is often difficult for a lot of people because they want to have what other people have. They want to have the newer vehicles, the bigger boat, the newest grill, or anything else. People like to have what their friends and neighbors have. However, one-factor people don't think about is that their friends and neighbors probably don't have financial freedom. Therefore, you want to take a moment to think about what is more important for you. Would you rather be in debt like your friends or you would rather have financial freedom?

5. Speak With a Financial Advisor

Sometimes, the best steps we can take when working towards financial freedom are talking with a financial advisor. They can often give up information, help us with a budget, make sure that we get the most out of our income, and tell us where we might be spending more money than we should. Furthermore, they can help you figure out what the best investments are, which are always helpful when looking at financial freedom. At the same time, they can help you plan for your retirement, which is one of the biggest ways you will remain financially free.

6. Completely Pay Off Your Credit Cards

If you are high-interest credit cards, which is often the case, you want to make sure that you pay these off every month. Therefore, your credit card spending should become part of your budget. What this means is you don't want to use your credit card for whatever you feel like. Instead, you want to create a list when you can and when you can't use your credit card. For example, you might agree that it is fine in emergencies or during Christmas shopping. You might also feel that you can use it during tips because it has trip insurance. Whatever you decide, you want to make sure you follow.

You also want to make sure that you pay off any high-interest loans. When it comes to loans that are lower in interest, they won't affect you too much.

7. Track Your Spending

Along with making sure you follow your budget, you also want to track your spending. There are several reasons for this. First, it will help you make sure that your budget is on track. We often forget about automatic bills paid monthly or don't realize how much we spend every month. These factors can make our budget off, which can cause an obstacle when you are working to reaching and keeping your financial freedom.

Fortunately, there are many apps that you can download, many of them are free, which will allow you to track your spending easily. Some of these apps include Mint or Personal Capital. These apps typically give you all the information you need. They will automatically tell you how much you are spending and how much income you still hold at the end of the month. Most of these apps will also give you charts to help you see your spending habits differently.

Remember The Best Habits to Reach Your Financial Freedom

CHAPTER 7:

Little Known Facts About Credit

Credit Cards Secrets Revealed

The first step when applying for a credit card is knowing the actual purpose why you are choosing to apply for a credit card in the first place. Some people find credit cards with cash reward to be very attractive. While other people may want to apply for a credit card offering a 12 to 18-month intro of 0% interest rate, so they can make purchases without paying interest for a specific time and take advantage of balance transfers. There are many more reasons why consumers apply for credit cards. Still, it is important to know the ins and outs about credit card so you can make well-informed decisions.

One of the most important things a consumer should know before applying for a credit card is their credit score. Understanding your credit score can put you in the driver's seat when you determine which is the best credit card for you. Consumers with excellent credit usually qualify for the best offers, but having average to poor credit often means a consumer will pay higher interest rates and possibly hefty annual fees.

Understanding Interest Rates

So, you recently applied for a credit card offering 0% for 6months, fast forward two weeks later you checked your mail and there it is your brand-new credit card with a $5000 limit. You are thrilled because you were planning on using the credit card to book a trip to Cancun and pay off the card over the next five months. So you wasted no time to book your ticket and hotel room; you also purchased things you think are necessary for your trips such as new clothes and shoes. Before long your credit card balance jumped up to $4,500, but not to worry about now because you are planning on paying off your debt before the six-month intro zero per cent grace period expires. Unfortunately, you were not able to pay off your credit card before the six-month interest grace period.

To make matters worse, you were only making a minimum payment of approximately $105 every month. But six months later your minimum payments were being applied to the interest and principal on your credit card balance, instead of being applied to just the principal balance. Therefore, if you were to keep making the minimum payment of $105 it would have taken you 56 months to pay off the credit card. You would have also paid approximately $1,280 in interest payments.

Annual Percentage Rate

When you initially applied for a credit card your annual percentage rate (APR) was 11.24%. However, what does this all mean to you? The APR is the annual cost of borrowing money from your credit card. The APR specifically applies to the interest rate that will be charged, if your credit card balance is not paid in full on or before the due date.

Types of APR

There are usually several types of APR that applies to your credit card account. For example, there is an APR for purchases. There is an APR for cash advance, balance transfers; an APR usually goes into effect when you make a late payment or violate any other terms of your credit card agreement.

Can My Credit Card Rate Increase?

Your credit card rate can increase if a promotional rate has expired. Your credit card rate can increase when you don't follow your credit card terms, when changes are made to a debt management plan and if your variable rate increases. What exactly is a debt management plan?

A debt management plan is an official agreement between a creditor and a debtor about a debt owed to the creditor by the debtor. The program is also designed to help the borrower pay off his or her outstanding debt faster. A debt management plan or debt relief plan is often a service a third-party company offers to someone who cannot afford to pay their debts on unsecured accounts. The third-party company (debt relief company) will collect the debtor's payment and then distribute it to the creditor. A debtor often uses a debt relief company because the company may help them evaluate their debt, help the debtor come up with a budget, establish a time frame to pay off their debt, and negotiate with creditors on their behalf.

A debtor usually enters into a debt management plan with a creditor when facing some financial hardship that makes it difficult for them to make even the minimum payments on their loan or credit card. The debt management plan will most likely include an agreement to allow the debtor to make an affordable payment to the creditor. The creditor will probably agree to dramatically reduce the interest rate on the debtor balance or outright eliminate the interest on the debtor balance.

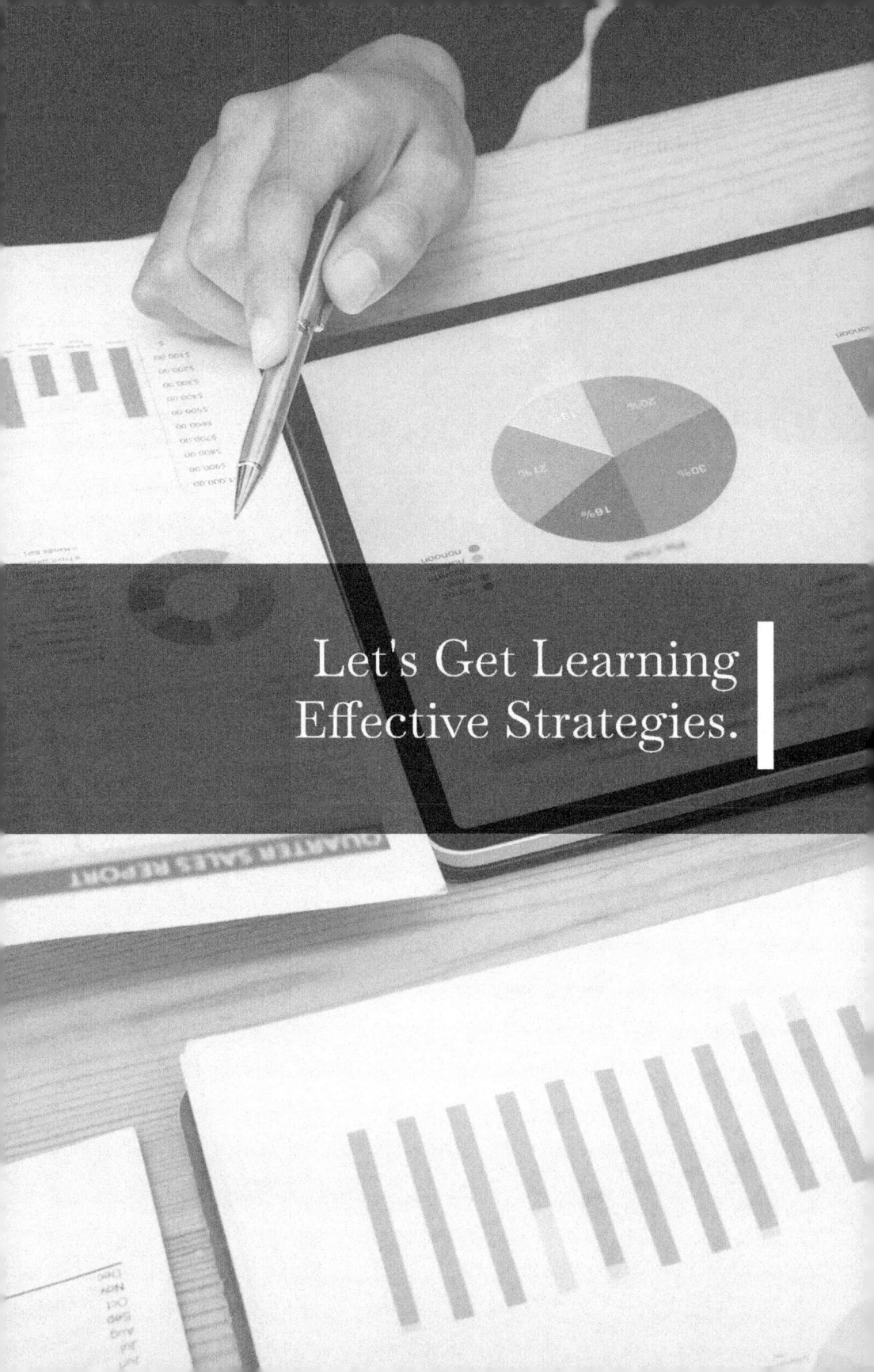

Let's Get Learning Effective Strategies.

CHAPTER 8:

Effective Strategies for Repairing your Credit

Pay to Delete Strategy

If you have derogatory items in your credit report, you can opt to pay the unpaid credit balance only if the creditor agrees to delete the items from your credit report. As I already mentioned, don't agree for a $0 balance appearing on your credit report since this taints your reputation. This will ultimately improve your rating. The idea is to ensure that whatever amount you agree to pay doesn't show up as your last activity date. If the creditor only cares about their money, why should they bother telling the world that you have finally paid?

In most instances, the creditors often write off debts within just 2 years of constant defaulting. This information is sold in bulk to a collection company for some pennies of a dollar. This means that the collection companies will even be just fine if you even pay a fraction of what you ought to pay. Whatever you pay, they will still make money! This makes them open to negotiations such as pay to delete since they have nothing to lose anyway.

- Therefore, only use the pay to delete approach at this level and not any other. The only other way around it for the collection company is a judgment, which can be costly, so you have some advantage here.
- Additionally, use this strategy when new negative items start showing up in your report that could hurt your reputation as a credit consumer.
- Also, since the creditors will often sell the same information to multiple collection companies, you might probably start noting the same debt reported by several companies; use pay to delete to get them off your report.
- You can also use this strategy if you have not successfully got items off your credit report using other methods. This is because opting to go the dispute way might only make the process cyclic, cumbersome, tiresome and frustrating; you don't want to get into this cycle.

Now that you know when to use this method, understanding how the entire process works is critical. To start with, ensure that you get an acceptance in writing if they agree to your times; don't pay without the letter! After you agree, allow about 45 days for the next credit report to be available to you by your credit monitoring service. These companies have the legal power to initiate the deletion process so don't accept anything less such as updating the balance; it is either a deletion or nothing. If they try to stall the process by saying that they cannot delete, mention that it will only take about 5 minutes to fill the Universal Data Form. Don't worry if one company does not agree with your terms since another one will probably show up and will gladly take the offer.

In any case, what do they have to gain when they keep your debt when you are willing to pay? Remember that the records will just be in your records for 7 years so since 2 years are already past, these companies have no choice otherwise you can simply let the 7 years pass! However, don't use this as an excuse for not paying your debts since the creditors can sue you to compel you to pay outstanding amounts. This process aims to ensure that whatever bad experience you have with one creditor doesn't make the others make unfavourable decisions on your part.

NOTE: don't be overly aggressive with creditors who have a lot to lose in the process especially the recent creditors since they can probably sue you. Your goal is only to be aggressive with creditors that are barred by the statute of limitation from suing you in court. You don't want to find yourself in legal trouble to add to your existing problems. Try and remain as smart as possible and make all the right moves to help you repair your credit at the earliest.

Pay to delete isn't the only option available to you; you can use other strategies to repair your credit.

Check for FDCPA (Fair Debt Collection Practices Act) Violations

The law is very clear on what collection agencies can do and what they cannot do as far as debt collection is concerned. For instance:

- They should not call you more than once in a day unless they can prove that their automated systems accidentally dialed it.
- They cannot call you before 8.00.am or after 9.00pm.
- They cannot threaten, belittle or yell at you to make you pay any outstanding debts.
- They cannot tell anyone else other than your spouse why they are contacting you.
- The best way to go about this is to let them know that you record all their calls.
- They cannot take more money from your account than you have authorized if they do an ACH.
- They are also not allowed to send you collection letters if you have already sent them a cease and desist order.

If you can prove that collection companies violate the laws, you should file a complaint with the company then have your lawyer send proof indicating the violations; you can then request that any outstanding debt be forgiven. You need to understand that the law is on your side in such circumstances;, if the violations are major, the collection companies could be forced to pay fines of up to $10,000 for these violations.

So, if your debt is significantly lower than this, you could be on your way to having your debt cleared since these companies would rather pay your debt than pay the fine. Every violation of the Fair Debt Collection Practices Act is punishable by a fine of up to $1000, which is payable to you. Don't just think of this as something that cannot amount to anything as far as repairing your credit is concerned.

Look for Errors on your Credit Reports

Your credit report should be free of errors. Even the slightest thing as reporting the wrong date of last activity on your credit report is enough to damage your credit. Suppose the write off date is different from what has been reported. In that case, you can dispute the entry to have it corrected to reflect that actual status of your credit. However, keep in mind that the credit bureaus will in most instances confirm that the negative entry is correct even if this is not the case, which means that they will not remove the erroneous item.

You must put in efforts to get them on the right track. To get them to comply, you have to inform them that the law requires them to have preponderance of their systems to ensure that these errors do not arise. Therefore, the mere fact of confirming the initial error is not enough. Inform them about the Notice (Summons) and complaint to let them understand that you are serious about the matter. Once they have an idea of your stance, they will put in efforts to do the right thing. The bureaus don't want any case to go to court since this could ultimately prove that their systems are weak or flawed, which means that they will probably be in some bigger problems.

So, try and drive a strong point across so that they understand you mean business. Mere exchange of emails will not do and you must send them details on how strong your case will be. This will make them understand their position and decide to help you avoid going to court. In turn, this will work to your advantage in making them dig deeper into the issue. However, this method will only work if you are confident that an error was made. You will also require proof for it and cannot merely state that there was an error.

Request Proof of The Original Debt

Suppose you are sure that the credit card has been written off for late payment. In that case, the carriers (Capital One and Citibank) likely cannot find the original billing statements within 30 days. They are required by the law to respond. This in effect allows you to have whatever entry you have disputed removed from the credit report as if it never happened.

Another handy approach is requesting the original contract that you signed to be provided to prove that you opened that particular credit card in the first instance. As you do this, don't just ask for "verification" since this only prompts the collection agency to "verify" that they received a request for collection on an account that has your name on it. Therefore, as a rule of thumb, ensure that you state clearly that you want them to provide proof of the debt including providing billing statements for the last several months and the original contract that you signed when opening the credit card account.

Pay the Original Creditor

When your debt is sold to collection agencies, you will probably risk having new items showing up on your credit report, which can further hurt your credit rating. However, you can stop that by sending a check with the full payment of any outstanding amount to the original creditor after which you just send a proof of payment to that collection agency and any other then request them to delete any derogatory items they have reported from your credit report.

It is always a good idea to be in direct contact with your creditor or creditors. In fact, many of these agencies will be fully equipped to cheat you and will follow through on plans to have your report show lousy credit scores. It is up to you to try and remove these "middlemen" and do the payment yourself. You could also enter into an agreement to pay a portion of the money to the creditor as full payment for the sum (the pay to delete strategy).

Under the federal law, if the original creditor accepts any payment as full payment for any outstanding debt, the collection agency has to remove whatever they have reported. This will only work if the original creditor accepts the price; it is possible for some of the checks you pay to the original creditor to be returned to you.

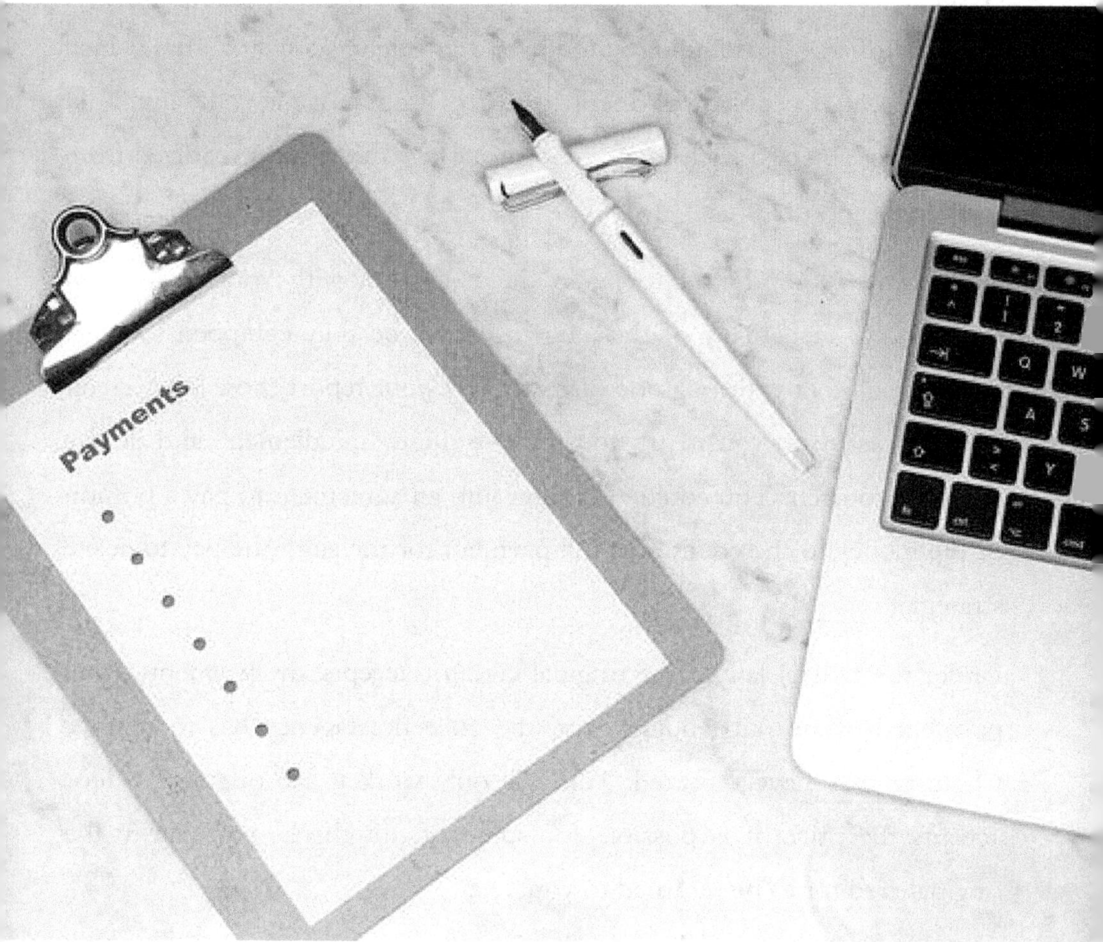
Payments

CHAPTER 9:

Controlling Various Kinds of Debt

Common Types of Debts

It depends on how you choose to see this. There are different kinds or types of debts. We will cut them into four groups to make this fun. Now, the first group.

1. Secured and Unsecured Loans.

Secured loans

> Secured loans are the types of debts you get by offering something as surety in case you don't pay that money up. As an example, if you are buying a house, a car, or getting a big work machine, you may opt for a loan when you don't have enough funds to clear the bills yourself. Often, that is a lot of money, and your credit company wants to be sure you're paying it all without complications. So, you are asked to mortgage some of your valued assets in turn. They keep the documents until your payment is complete. If you don't pay up, there are a few legal actions to

make, and they sell the assets. The norm is that you take this type of loan on significant investments.

Unsecured loans

Unsecured loans are the direct opposite of secured loans. You do not have to stake anything to access a loan like this. All you need is indicate your interest, submit your essential documents, and the loan is yours. The type of loan you're asking for is what determines what you will be offering. For example, your credit report may be enough to get you another credit card. You may have to drop a little deposit plus your credit report when you're signing up for some utilities. All of these have a small or minimal risk by the user. Only that you can cover simple services with this type of loan, no more. Now, you can imagine which weighs higher on a credit score ranked by FICO.

2. Fixed and Revolving Payment Method

Fixed Payment Method

A lot of times, your credit company lays out clear terms, duration, and method of payment to you. When this happens, we say you have got a fixed payment method. Usually, fixed payment methods attract fixed interests too. When you take part in a dealership deal, for example, you may be graced to get that money paid at a particular amount each month and a particular interest rate. Say, the car is worth a thousand USD. You are allowed to pay up in two years, with a total interest of 30%. That is pretty straightforward, right? That's just how fixed payment loans work. A mortgage is an example of fixed payment loans, so you might say they are pretty standard.

Revolving Payment Method:

These types of loans are those that swing like unpredictable bells. There are no exact modalities on most items. You simply take the loans and pay as you can. For example, you can pay when you have the funds; there is no exact deadline for payments. You don't get a limit to interest rates too. Often, your utility, as well as your credit card, fall into this category. This is the exact reason you draw up a credit card, and you can use the credit card as much as you like each month. You don't have to pay up that money when the month ends. You can pay a little now, a lot more over the coming months. But as FICO had earlier advised, it makes perfect sense to draw up only 30% or less of your credit limits. Expectedly, your interest rate is determined by how promptly you clear off that debt.

3. Good and Bad Loans

No questions, this list can't be closed if this group isn't here.

The Good Loans

Classifying loans as good or bad does not exist in official records. Maybe if it did, nobody would ever be excited to try out the bad ones. In any case, a right loan is any loan drawn to invest in resources that may become useful and available over a long period, sometimes, forever. Some of them are:

Mortgage: If it is damning to size up your mortgage and you are planning to hand over the building, my sincere suggestion is that you keep pulling through, and you remain upbeat. This is one of the loans you can't ever regret taking. It is glaring to anyone that houses are assets that you don't use up any moment soon. A home may get into a bad shape sometimes. That's normal. You are expected to keep it brimming with brightness naturally. If you do things right, you can't ever have to pay rents. You also have an asset you can risk getting considerable loans to build your career. If things get worse, you can auction the house and restart your careers somewhere. However, you choose to see it, a loan drawn to get a home is a good one. Just be sure you can keep paying till the end before drawing the loan at all.

Student Loans: Well, you might hear someone say drawing student loan in insane. But if you look over the sayings, you'd have something different. You've got to get a good education, and you can't afford it at that moment. It makes perfect sense to tangle yourself in a loan, bag that degree, and pay back much more quickly. As you may fear, your first few years after school would be spent clearing your old debt. But you become free soon, and you'd have access to opportunities you may not have found without top training. From all viewpoints you see this, it is a win-win for all teams. So, I'd vote this as a right loan!

Business: Now, this is another perspective. If you are getting the loans to jack up your investments, you are settling for a good one too. It is undoubtedly a risk, since the business may pick up and may not. But if you probably play your cards right, your business can boom, and that is the start of a goal you didn't see coming.

So, Bad Loans?

Auto loans: For a fact, you must be curious to know why auto loans should be tagged a bad debt, isn't it? I bet! Well, it is. Auto Loans, dealerships, and whatever kind of car loan you get into is a bad loan. This is because cars are not assets that can be used for a long while. If you sign a two or five-year loan deal, your car is already developing some sorts of problems. So, you'd have to spend on it, and at that same time, pay your auto loans. It would be a mess in a few years.

Credit Card Loans: Credit Card Loans are probably the worst you can take. They can't be used to get important stuff. And either you take note or not, your debt is on the rise with every month you forgot to clear up.

Most Other loans: Most of the other types of loans fall into this category, especially those you draw from friends and family. They are often not precisely significant and should be avoided. Except, of course, they are critical to you, and you are sure there's some way you can quickly pay it all back.

How to Control Your Credit

Regardless of what credit types you have drawn, it is vital to monitor and control it all before it gets out of hand. Even if it's slipped a bit, the best option you've got is to find some way to monitor and control it. Hence, I'll be showing you some easy and practical ways in the next few lines. Here;

1. Don't let things slip off: That's the first rule. Prevention is way better than cure. It stands to reason that if you can plan appropriately and watch out for sinking moments, you shouldn't have to fight to save your credit score fiercely. All you need is to do the math. Where are you heading to? What are your chances of hitting it big or terribly crashing? What would you have to do to avoid falling into a debt pit and

struggling to pay up? Several things we might say. Your first job is to find those targets and set them working.

2. Don't spend payments: Pending payments only increase your penalties. Whether for fixed and revolving debts. So, with the facts that you should avoid pending your payments. Clear them off the instant you are able to.

3. Don't toy with revolving debts: Revolving debts are full of surprises. You would usually assume they are the littlest, and so, they can be paid after the much bigger debts. In reality, your revolving debts (like your credit cards) cart away more than your fixed debts. They tend to increase all the time, and there's a high potential for interest increase too, which doesn't happen in fixed credit cases. Hence, it washes that you should pay them up before considering some other debts at all. Don't delay others too!

If you do the math and your revolving debts are out, you will have a concrete idea of how to tackle the only other debts you have left. This itself is an acute style of controlling debts that you didn't notice. Now you know, cheers.

CHAPTER 10:

Guaranteed Methods to Protect Credit Score

Do Not Fully Use Your Credit Cards

30% of your score is how you use your credit. For example, having a credit card with a $10,000 limit is amazing! You can do whatever you want with it, and trust me, that is something I often did. But, that is actually another item that can gravely affect your credit score. You want to make sure you are only using up to 30% of your credit card. "But Alan, what is the point of having a $10,000 card limit if I can only use $3,000?!" Great question! Let me explain it in more detail. By the end of the billing month, you only want to have, at most, 30% on your credit card balance. You can use the full amount of the credit card if you want, just pay it off before the end of the billing month.

A simple and fun example goes like this, I want to be a baller and buy 500 large pizzas for a block party, at the cost of $15 each (and I was in some weird loophole where taxes were exempt, I would have placed $7,500 on my credit card, even though I already had $2000 on my card. That is clearly 95% of my card limit! But, if I turned around and paid everything off my credit card, the end of my billing month would show that I had $2,000 debt. My credit score will not be negatively affected by buying food for the best block party in existence! Now, in a perfect world, paying off your cards in its entirety by the end of the billing month is by far the best thing you can do. Pay what you can but stay under 30%!

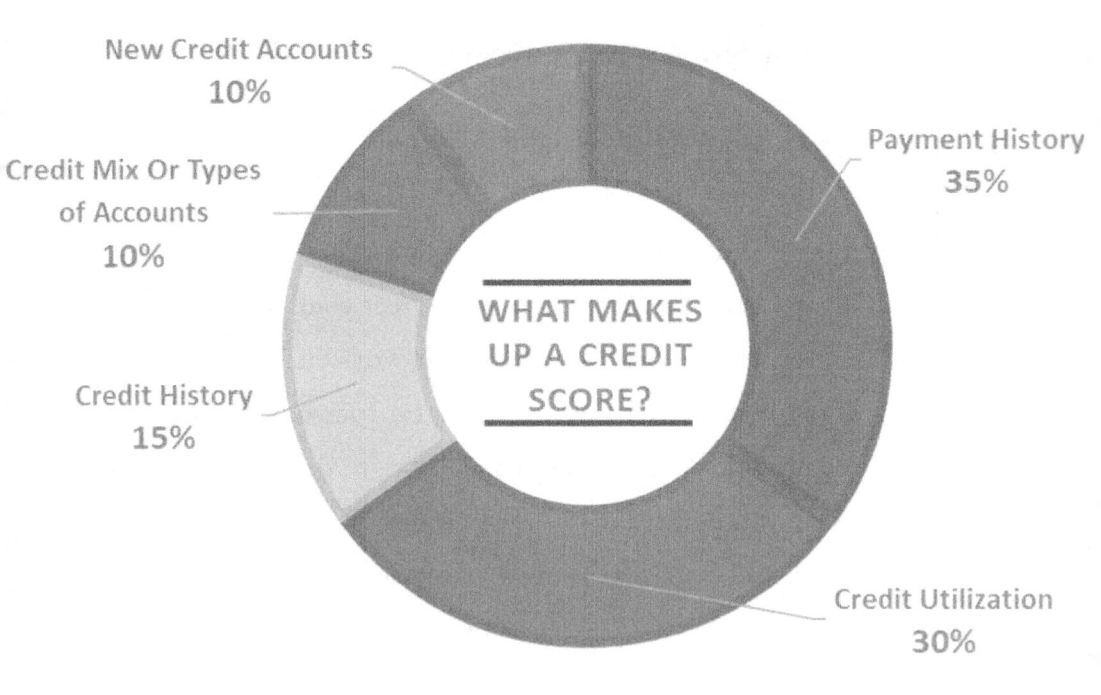

New Credit Accounts 10%

Credit Mix Or Types of Accounts 10%

Credit History 15%

WHAT MAKES UP A CREDIT SCORE?

Payment History 35%

Credit Utilization 30%

Hacking Your Way to That Perfect Score

The below image is a fantastic simple guide to climbing up that credit score ladder. Now, that looks nice, but what exactly is considered "excellent" credit? Well, after searching and searching, it seems as though you are considered Excellent, when your credit score reaches 760. That number seems to be the number that is in the goldilocks zone in the credit score world. With an Excellent credit score rating, you will have the best interest rates, you will have the least amount of issues attempting to get loans, and you most definitely will never have to leave a deposit whenever you want to turn on your utilities at the brand new home you will buy with that amazing mortgage rate you will get!

Ask Sebby	Excellent	Good	Fair	Poor	Very Poor
Credit Card Utilization (High)	0-9%	10-29%	30-49%	50-74%	75%+
Payment History (High)	100%	99%	98%	97%	<97%
Derogatory Marks (High)	0	-	1	2-3	4+
Age of Credit History (Medium)	9+ years	7-8 years	5-6 years	2-4 years	< 2 years
Total Accounts (Low Impact)	21+	11-20	-	6-10	0-5
Credit Inquiries (Low Impact)	0	1-2	3-4	5-8	9+

We need to make sure we cover everything. If you have missed/late payment marks on your credit report, reach out to that credit card company and ask them to get them removed! Let them know of the reason why you were not able to pay them on time and then let them know of the good standing you are with them while letting them know of your goals of improving your credit score. I have gotten 3 late payment marks taken off within a month!

If you had collection marks on your credit report, and you went through the process of trying to remove them and you still ended up paying, wait a few months and send them a letter asking to get it removed. This may work. But if you really want it to work, send a lot of letters, 2-3 a week until someone who gets paid $10 an hour does not want to deal with it anymore and removes the mark from the credit report. I have done it once, and though at first, I felt shameful, 3 months later I no longer had it! I must have broken through to someone! Win!

If you are new to getting credit, having 9-year worth of credit history will definitely be a difficult task, you may have to wait. But in that time, follow this guide and make sure you are making all your payments on time! For those of you who have been around for quite some time, do not close your credit cards. If you have to, then please be wary, but I would hold onto any and all credit cards and never close them. If you do not want to use them anymore, just don't use them.

CHAPTER 11:

The Credit Bureau

Credit bureaus are privately held, billion-dollar organizations whose primary reason for existing is to make cash; that is what revenue driven organizations do right? They keep data that lenders furnish them - regardless of whether accurate or inaccurate - about our credit association with them and sell it. Basic, right? This straightforward plan of action generates over $4 Billion per year!

One wellspring of income for them originates from selling the information on our credit reports to different lenders, managers, insurance agencies, credit card organizations - and whoever else you approve to see your credit information. In addition to the fact that they provide them with crude data; yet they likewise sell them various methods for examining the data to decide the risk of stretching out credit to us. In addition to trading our information to lenders, they likewise sell our information to us - credit scores, credit observing administrations, extortion security, wholesale fraud prevention - interestingly enough this region has quickly gotten perhaps the greatest wellspring of income. Furthermore, those pre-endorsed offers in our letter drop each week, or garbage mail? That's right; they got our information from the credit bureaus as well. Organizations buy in to an assistance provided by the three credit bureaus that sell them a rundown of consumer's credit information that fit a pre-decided criterion.

Presently, as opposed to prevalent thinking, credit bureaus don't have any contribution on whether you ought to be endorsed for a loan or not; that is absolutely based on the credit criteria of the lender you're working with. However, by utilizing the entirety of the information that has been set on your credit report (personal information, payment history, and credit propensities) and FICO's technique for scoring that data, they do tell them with how creditworthy you are.

What Credit Bureaus Do?

Credit bureaus collect information from various sources in accordance with consumer information. The activity is done for various reasons and includes data from singular consumers. Included is the information concerning a people charge payments and their getting. Utilized for evaluating creditworthiness, the information provides lenders with an outline of your accounts if a loan repayment is required. The interest rates charged on a loan are additionally worked out concerning the kind of credit score shown by your experience. It is thusly not a uniform procedure, and your credit report is the significant instrument that affects future loans.

Based on risk-based valuing, it pegs various risks on the various customers in this manner deciding the cost you will acquire as a borrower. Done as credit rating, it is an assistance provided to various interested parties in the public. Terrible credit histories are affected for the most part by settled court commitments which mark you for high interest rates every year. Duty liens and bankruptcies, for example, shut you out of the conventional credit lines and may require a great deal of arrangement for any loan to be offered by the bank.

Bureaus collect and examine credit information including financial data, personal information, and elective data. This is given by various sources generally marked data furnishers. These have an exceptional association with the credit bureaus. An average gathering of data furnishers would comprise of creditors, lenders, utilities, and debt collection agencies. Pretty much any association which has had payment involvement in the consumer is qualified including courts. Any data collected for this situation is provided to the credit bureaus for grouping. When it is accumulated, the data is placed into specific repositories and files claimed by the bureau. The information is made accessible to customers upon request. The idea of such information is important to lenders and managers.

The information is in this manner material in various conditions; credit evaluation andbusiness thought are simply part of these. The consumer may likewise require the information to check their individual score and the home proprietor may need to check their inhabitants report before renting an apartment. Since the market is saturated by borrowers, the scores will, in general, be robotic. Straightforward examination would deal with this by giving the client a calculation for speedy appraisal. Checking your score once every other year should deal with errors in your report.

Individuals from the public are qualified for one free credit report from every one of the significant bureaus. This is organized in the Fair Credit Report Act, FCTA. Other government rules associated with the assurance of the consumer incorporate Fair and Accurate Credit Transaction Act, Fair Credit Billing Act and Regulation B. Statutory bodies have additionally been made for the regulation of the credit bureaus. The Fair-Trade Commission serves to as a controller for the consumer credit report agencies while the Office of the Comptroller of Currency fills in as a manager of all banks going about as furnishers.

Choose A Debt Payoff Method That Works For You

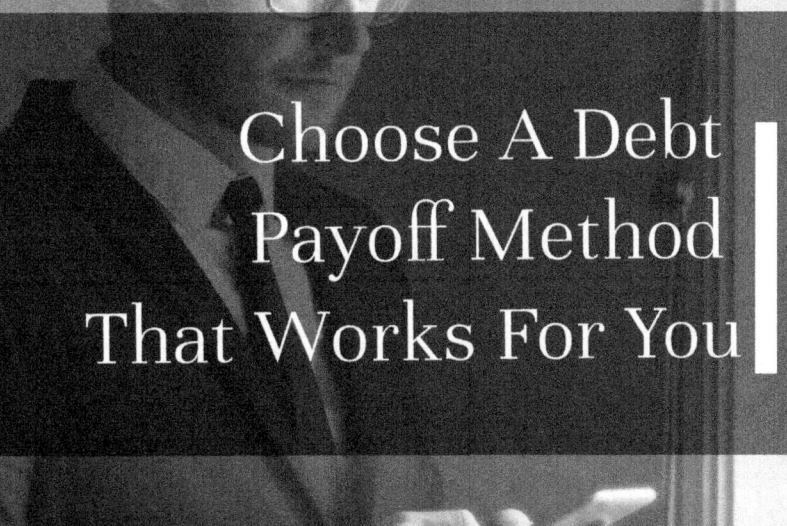

CHAPTER 12:

How to Overcome Credit Card Debt

What is a Credit Card Debt?

When you incur a credit card debt, you actually keep borrowing money every month, and that is why it is also known as revolving debt. But it is only good until you have the capacity to repay them but when you can't, the debt keeps accumulating. When compared to the loan accounts, you can actually keep using your credit card accounts for an indefinite period of time. On the other hand, in the case of instalment loan accounts, after you have cleared out the entire balance, the account will be closed.

Another thing that you should keep in mind about a credit card debt is that it is an unsecured type of debt. In simpler terms, there is nothing that the company can seize, like a house or a card, even when you have failed to repay them. But yes, if you are not able to repay the money you borrowed from the credit card, it is going to affect your credit score drastically.

How Is Credit Card Debt Accumulated?

When you get a credit card, you will see that there will be a due date within which you have to clear the entire balance that you have accumulated on your credit card, and if you fail to do so, you will be accumulating debt. There is a term called APR or Annual Percentage Rate and this is a rate of interest that is charged on your debt when it keeps accumulating one month after the other. The APR that you will be charged may not be the same with someone else's and this is because it keeps differing with your credit history, the bank issuer, and the type of card that you have.

The benchmark fed funds rate of the Federal Reserve and the prime rate of the credit card interests is somewhat tied, and that is the average value. The credit card debt will increase or decrease with respect to any changes in the target rate made by the Fed.

Now, I want to give you an even clearer picture of how this debt accumulates. For starters, there is a minimum payment that you will have to pay every month whenever you use your credit card to make purchases. This payment is calculated based on a certain percentage (with some additional interest charges) of your balance. If you pay this amount in full, then well and good, but if you don't, then you will be liable to interest. So, the interest will increase if you pay even lesser. The reason behind this is that the nature of credit card interests is compounding so the interest keeps accruing. Thus, if you take a longer time to clear off the debts, then you will owe a huge amount of money to the company, which is much more than what you owed before.

What Happens After 7 Years?

This is basically a time limit until which a record is shown in a credit report. But there are certain other negative issues that will stay in your credit report even after seven years, for example, certain judgments, tax liens that are unpaid, and bankruptcy.

But you also have to keep in mind that if any debt is unpaid, then it is not exactly going to vanish even after seven years. Even if the credit report does not list it, you will still owe that money to the lender.

There are several other legal ways that can be implemented by the lenders, creditors, and debt collectors to collect the debt that you haven't paid. Some of these methods include a court giving permission to garnish your wages, sending letters, calling you, and so on. In some cases, you can even be sued.

One thing that you benefit because of this seven- years rule is that when the debt is no longer visible on your credit report, it cannot affect your credit score. Thus, you can actually have a better chance of gaining back a good score. Another thing to keep in mind is that this seven-years term is only for the negative information on your report and not the position information because they will stay on the report forever. You should keep an eye out after the seven- year mark as to whether the credit bureaus have removed that information or not. They usually do it automatically, but in case they don't then you will have to raise a dispute.

Many people have this question of what happens to their debt if they accidentally die. Well, in that case, it will be your estate that will be used to pay the debt off. Remember that the debt will not be shoved in someone else's hand in your family because whatever money you owe, it is your debt and not anyone else's. And so, whatever you had, like your accounts and assets will then be used for clearing the debt. And after that, if anything remains from your assets, your heir will receive it.

How to Eliminate Credit Card Debt?

Now that you have a basic idea of what a credit card debt is, let us talk about how you can eliminate it.

Start Eliminating High-Interest Debts First

When you are trying to eliminate your credit card debt, the biggest obstacle that will stand in your way are the ones that carry a very high rate of interest. Sometimes, the rate of interest can even be in double- digits, sometimes as high as 22%. In that case, paying it off can be a really difficult task. But the reason why I am asking you to start eliminating them first because when you will have cleared these debts, you will have a greater amount of money left in your hand at the end of each month.

Another thing that you could do, but only if you have enough credit available, is to apply for a new credit card. But this should be a zero-interest one. Once you get it, transfer the balance to eliminate the high-interest debt. Yes, I know that some of you might be thinking that it is not a sensible thing to do to apply for another credit card and that is why I will be asking you to get it only if you think you have enough self- restraint not to buy a bunch of stuff that you don't need.

Keep Making Small Payments

Quite contrary to the technique I mentioned above is another technique which is called the snowflake technique. With this process, you will be making small payments towards your debt every time you get some extra cash in hand. Whatever payment you are making, it does not matter as long as you keep paying.

You can pay $10, or you can pay $20 but at the end of the year, you will find that you have reduced about $1000 simply by paying such small amounts almost every day, even if you are paying $2 on any day.

People often ignore this method, thinking that it will be only small amounts but you should not make the mistake of overlooking these small amounts as they have quite the power in them. When you are making these small payments, it would feel as if they are not even leaving any dent but with time, they will sum up and cause a considerable effect on your debt.

Preventive Measures to Avoid Credit Card Debt

Have an Emergency Fund

Think about a situation when you have encountered a problem that requires you to spend a lot of money, for example, a car repair or job loss or medical emergencies. In such a situation, what you need is an emergency fund, but when people don't have that, they resort to credit cards for help.

But why arrive at such a situation when you can build an emergency fund that will cover at least six months' expenses. If you are finding it difficult to come up with a huge amount, then start by accumulating $500 and then work your way up to $1000. A fund of this size will help you to figure out any small expenses that crop up overnight. Take your time to build your emergency fund so that you do not have to rely on debt ever.

But Only Those Things That You Can Afford

When you have a credit card in hand, it can get really tempting, and you start buying whatever you think you want. But take a step back and think whether you can really afford that item if you did not have a credit card. If not, then don't buy it now. Make a goal to save the money required for purchasing that item instead of buying it on credit.

Don't Transfer Balance If Not Necessary

Some people have this habit of clearing their balance with a higher credit card but such repeated balance transferring can actually backfire at you. When you keep transferring balanced without keeping track of your activities, you might end up with an ever- increasing balance and you will also have to clear the fee requires for all those transfers.

Try Not Taking Out a Cash Advance

Sometimes, you may be in the moment, and you were not thinking clearly so, you decide to take a cash advance. But you have to remember and remind yourself that a cash advance comes with very hefty transaction fees and you are not even going to get a grace period in which you can avoid the charges. Moreover, you will have to realize that you are getting into credit card debt if you have started making cash advanced. The moment you see it happening, you will have to start working on that emergency fund and also tweak your budget.

Lastly, I would like to say that no matter how many measures you take, try avoiding increasing your credit cards unnecessarily because the more the number of credit cards, the more you will have to stop yourself from overspending.

CHAPTER 13:

Credit Repair from Scratch

How to Build a Credit Score from scratch?

There are several ways and all of them are effective.

1. The first is to open a bank account. Having an account open will not increase your score, but it will give you a starting point to show regular income. After a few months, you can ask your bank (remember to show off your best smile) what services they offer to increase your Credit Score. My bank, for example, offers a mini-loan of $ 500 tied up to be returned in 6 months. It means that you deposit $ 500, they re-loan them to you at a favorable rate and when, in 6 months, you finish paying the instalments, they give you back the $ 500 in the barrel. Practically in 6 months, you paid interest as a "tax" with the sole purpose of accumulating points. To put it in simpler words: from 500 and 500 you return, then you pay 500 in instalments + interest and you return 500 at the end. It is an expense, but this type of loan guarantees you a considerable accumulation of points, but only if you are regular in payments.

2.	The second, and in my opinion the best, is to apply for a Secured Credit Card. Unlike traditional credit cards, you do not have to show any kind of entry to get approval, but you also have a usage limit. The only thing required is a deposit which is returned to you after a year of regular use. Until a couple of years ago, the deposit was around 200 euros, but with the debt problems that developed after the recession, all the major credit companies have lowered the costs. For example, I applied with Capital One (but there are many others like Discover). The deposit was only $ 49 and the card limit was $ 200 a month with the option of 2% cash back on gas or restaurant expenses. I started using it regularly every month ONLY for these two things and, after a year, my Credit Score was already considered very good, they also returned the deposit and the cash back and the credit limit rose to 500 dollars after only six months. We clarify that you are not obliged to use it only for these things, but I have limited myself for two reasons. The first is to accumulate cash back (i.e. a refund) at the end of the year. The second is to make sure I never use more than 30% of the card limit. Which brings me to the next point.

3.	Never exceed 30% of the credit card limit. Believe it or not, it is essential that you show that you do not need a credit card to pay for your things, but that you use it only when strictly necessary or as an accurate choice. The more you use it constantly the better, but judiciously.

4.   Pay your instalments regularly. All the above points have absolutely no value if you are not constant in payments. No one here scales your loan or credit card debts from your salary. It is your responsibility to remember when you have to pay or set up an automatic payment from your bank account. I decided to set up automatic payments. As long as he has a good memory, you never know what can happen that can put you off your mind on the expiry day. So, I strongly suggest you do the same because even a missed payment will negatively affect your score.

5.   Vary the types of debt as much as you can. If you can make the Secured Card And the mini-loan with the bank at the same time, do it. The more options you have, the faster your Credit Score will grow. Of course, always keep in mind that if you don't pay on time, they show up at home with the Pit bulls (so to speak or almost). So, if you're not sure you can do better, don't risk it and wait a little longer.

6.   Add your name to someone else's credit card as an "authorized user". If, for example, if you are married to an American who has had much more time than you to accumulate a decent score (as in my case), it might be a good idea for him to indicate you as an authorized user of his credit cards. This does not mean that you will actually have to use his credit cards, but the more his score improves, the more he will positively influence yours. Be careful though! If you go down, he comes down with you. This type of choice involves a fat, large demonstration of trust so be

careful not to betray it. If you mess up the Credit Score that has been sweating so much since he was in swaddling clothes, well I wouldn't want to be in your shoes!

7.   Check your Credit Score regularly to make sure there are no problems you are unaware of and have such nasty surprises. Even a late paid bill can affect your payer profile. Now pay attention to the following because it's important. There are several ways to check where you are with the economic 'pregnancy'. The first is to apply here for your Annual Credit Report, but you are entitled to a free check only once a year. The second is to check directly in Credit Bureaus such as Trans union, Equifax or Experian. Also in these cases, you can have a free check per year, or pay a monthly instalment to keep your score constantly under control. Obviously, the annual checks have their advantages, but be careful not to take too much advantage of their services. Believe it or not, every time you request a check this will lower your Credit Score. Crazy, right? And this brings me to the only sensible solution that remains to keep the score under control.

8.   Download the free Credit Karma app. Not only does it constantly give you a detailed report of your score, but also what has positively or negatively influenced, which credit cards or loans are best suited to your situation, your progress, and many other functions. It's all free and, although not updated to the minute, rather accurate. It does not lower your

Credit Score and also offers you many other services such as online and free tax returns. Due to Credit Karma, other major credit companies have also had to adjust to offer the Credit Score free check. For example, Capital One and Discover have now integrated this service into their offers (although in a more limited way being a cost to them).

If you follow these tips in a year you can afford to ask for a car loan without having to pay disproportionate interest or even more, depending on your income and your general receivables/payables situation. This reminds me of how important it is to start as soon as possible. Remember that this is the first thing they look at when you need to apply for a loan!

Conclusion

One of the tools you can use to your advantage is the free investment or personal loan; however, it has certain restrictions. Never buy a car with this type of credit, since there is a specific credit for it. A car loan has more convenient interest rates and benefits than a personal loan. It is also not good for paying off another credit, except for the famous "debt purchase". Don't enter the so-called "carousel", in other words, do not take out one loan to pay off another, unless it is a debt consolidation: take out a loan to pay off several debts and keep just one. It is also not recommended to complete the down payment on a home loan; always save for that type of purchase.

You shouldn't lend to other people; even though you know them, they're not you and they can probably fail to pay on time. Easier to repay that loan? Get lower rates by opening an account in the chosen entity, especially if it is an account where your credits are saved; you would have access to lower interest rates. It helps to have a credit card from that entity. A good way to reduce interest on your loan is to pay extraordinary fees, that is, pay double fees in some month and generate savings. Remember: having pre-approved loans and cards is a good indicator in your credit history; for different entities, you are a low risk person and you have a solvent economic situation.

If you are denied of getting a credit, is maybe because it exceeds your possibility to pay or maybe you cannot prove that you have enough incomes to pay for it. Ask for the reason of the denial. In this way, you will be able to see the improvements you can make, such as reducing your debts and pending loans to settle, increasing your income for a greater possibility to pay, or revisiting your credit report to request again the amount to be borrowed.

These habits will allow you to improve financially, while your credit history benefits.

You must save money. If you want to see your money grow, you have to make sacrifices. Find all the ways to make a living. Let me give you an example. I have a coach, who warned me that two health conditions are the most expensive: coronary heart disease and mental health-related illnesses. Even if you have a humble job, you will have to save for one or both conditions. I won't tell you which one I have, but I can assure you that the cost of medicines and private medical consultation is high.

Quit the job you have. Currently, a stable job in some countries is not secure. There are many graduated people in my profession and every day there are more staff cuts in the workplaces. Entrepreneurship is the key. As an example, from my parents, my mother is obstetrician and my dad is an electronic technician and chauffeur. One day they stopped being employees of the government and started several entrepreneurships: private transportation, a convenience store, food concessionaire, lender, home installations. These ventures have brought them more income than their careers. Today, they continue to invest in real estate while receiving residual income from rentals of apartments and shops.

One of my grandparents worked in a textile factory for 40 years as a machine technician. Even though he bought two houses he worked for 40 years. He worked even on holidays, didn't saw his family as much as he wanted to and had to rest after so many years of work. I particularly, bid farewell to an expensive lifestyle: I bid farewell to that pitcher with the head of a cat and to that luxurious first-class journeys. Finally: Bill Gates, Steve Jobs, Michael Dell, left their comfortable life and set out on their own path. And you, what do you need to start creating your financial freedom? It's up to you.

Dave R. W. Graham

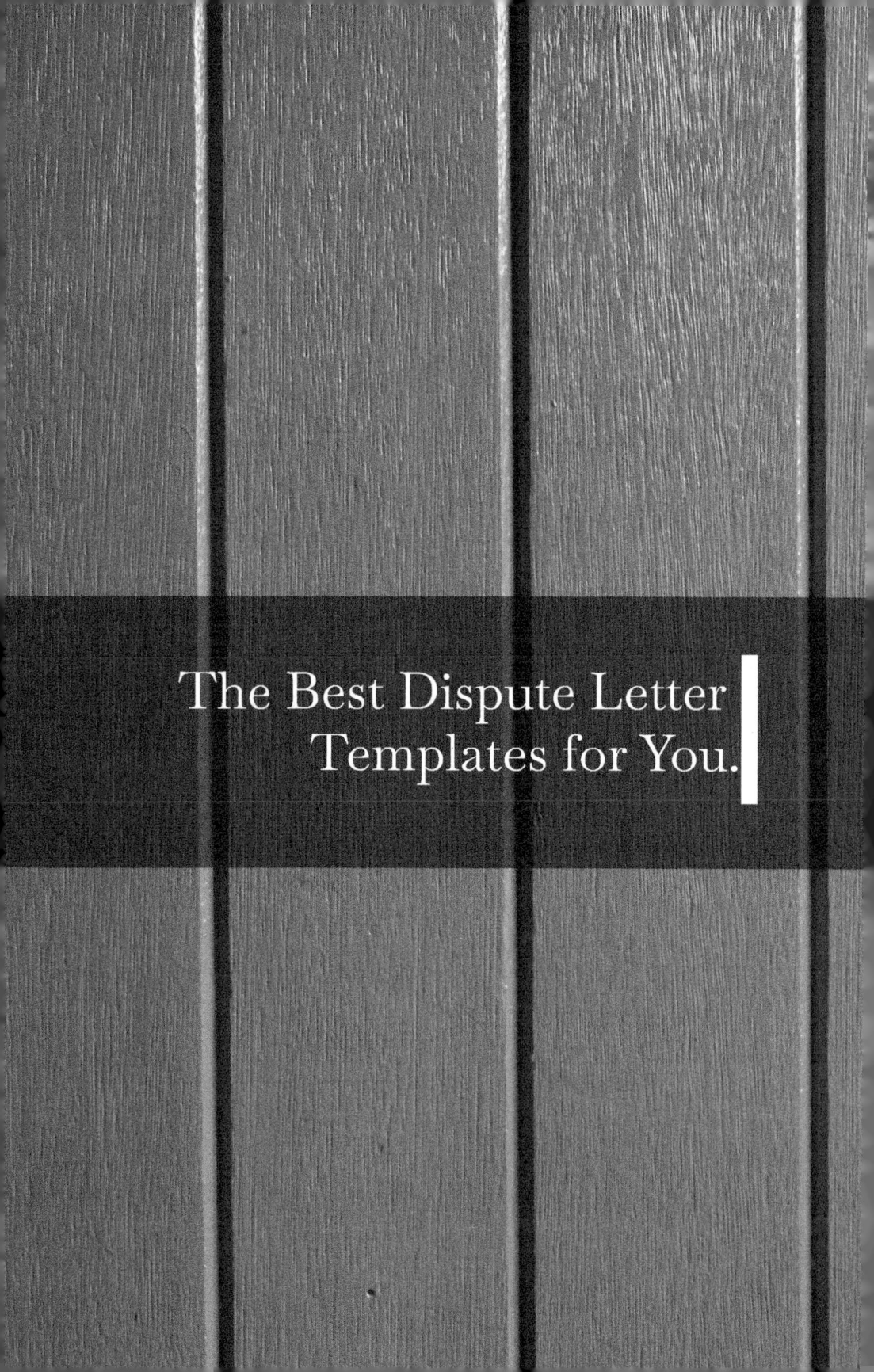

The Best Dispute Letter Templates for You.

BONUS:

The Best Templates You Can Use to Work with Section 609

Dispute Letter Templates

Letter 1: Affidavit of unknown inquiries

EQUIFAX
P.O. box 740256
ATLANTA GA 30374

My name Is John William; my current address is 6767. W Phillips Road, San Jose, CA 78536, SSN: 454-02-9928, Phone: 415-982-3426, Birthdate: 6-5-1981

I checked my credit reports and noticed some inquiries from companies that I did not give consent to access my credit reports, I am very concerned about all activity going on with my credit reports these days. I immediately demand the removal of these inquiries to avoid any confusion as I DID NOT initiate these inquires or give any form of consent

Dave Robert Warren Graham

electronically, in person, or over the phone. I am fully aware that without permissible purpose no entity is allowed to pull my credit unless otherwise noted in section 604 of the FCRA.

The following companies did not have permission to request my credit report:

CUDL/FIRST CALIFORNIA ON 6-15-2017

CUDL/NASA FEDERAL CREDIT UNION ON 6-15-2017

LOANME INC 3-14-2016

CBNA on 12-22-2017

I once again demand the removal of these unauthorized inquiries immediately.

(Signature)

THANK YOU

Letter 2: Affidavit of suspicious addresses

1-30-2018

ASHLEY WHITE

2221 N ORANGE AVE APT 199

FRESNO CA 93727

PHONE: 559-312-0997

SSN: 555-59-4444

BIRTHDATE: 4-20-1979

EQUIFAX

P.O. box 740256

ATLANTA GA 30374

To whom it may concern:

I recently checked a copy of my credit report and noticed some addresses reporting that do not belong to me or have been obsolete for an extended period of time. For the safety of my information, I hereby request that the following obsolete addresses be deleted from my credit reports immediately;

4488 N white Ave apt 840 Fresno, CA 93722

4444 W Brown Ave apt 1027 Fresno CA 93722

13330 E Blue Ave Apt 189 Fresno CA 93706

DAVE ROBERT WARREN GRAHAM

I have provided my identification card and social security card to verify my identity and current address. Please notify any creditors who may be reporting any unauthorized past accounts that are in connection with these mentioned addresses as I have exhausted all of my options with the furnishers.

(Your signature)

This letter is to get a response from the courts to show the credit bureaus that you have evidence that they cannot legally validate the Bankruptcy

Letter 3: Affidavit of James Robert

U.S BANKRUPTCY COURT
700 STEWART STREET 6301
SEATTLE, WA 98101
RE: BANKRUPTCY (164444423TWD SEATTLE, WA)

To whom it may concern:

My Name is JAMES ROBERT my mailing address is 9631 s 2099h CT Kent, WA 99999.

I recently reviewed my credit reports and came upon the above referenced public record. The credit agencies have been contacted and they report in their investigation that you furnished or reported to them that the above matter belongs to me. This act may have violated federal and Washington state privacy laws by submitting such information directly to the credit agencies, Experian, Equifax, and Trans Union via mail, phone or fax.

I wish to know if your office violated Washington State and federal privacy laws by providing information on the above referenced matter via phone, fax or mail to Equifax, Experian or Trans Union.

Please respond as I have included a self-addressed envelope,

Thank You (your signature)

Letter 4: Affidavit for account validation

First letter you send to the credit bureaus for disputes

1-18-2019

TRANSUNION

P.O. BOX 2000

CHESTER PA 19016

To Whom It May Concern:

My name is John Doe, SSN:234-76-8989, my current address is 4534. N Folk street Victorville, CA 67378, Phone: 310-672-0929 and I was born on 4-22-1988.

After checking my credit report, I have found a few accounts listed above that I do not recognize. I understand that before any account or information can be furnished to the credit bureaus; all information and all accounts must be 100% accurate, verifiable and properly validated. I am not disputing the existence of this debt, but I am denying that I am the responsible debtor. I am also aware that mistakes happen, I believe these accounts can belong to someone else with a similar name or with my information used without my consent either from the furnisher itself or an individual.

I am demanding physical documents with my signature or any legally binding instruments that can prove my connection to these erroneous entries, Failure to fully verify that these accounts are accurate is a violation of the FCRA and must be removed or it will continue to damage my ability to obtain additional credit from this point forward.

I hereby demand that the accounts listed above be legally validated or be removed from my credit report immediately.

Thank You (Your signature)

Dave Robert Warren Graham

Letter 5: Sample Dispute Letter to Credit Bureaus

Date

(Sent certified mail with a return receipt requested)

Your Name

Your Address

Your City, State, Zip Code

( ) Insert name of bureau: Equifax, Experian, or Trans Union

Address

City, State, Zip Code

To Whom It May Concern:

This letter is to request that you investigate inaccurate information contained in my ( ) credit file. (Fill in the blank with Equifax, Experian, or Trans Union, depending on the credit bureau to which you are writing.) The information I am disputing pertains to the ( ) of the account listed below: (Fill in the blank with the word "ownership" or "status," depending on the type of dispute.)

( ) Account, with the account number ending as ( ) (Put the account name and the last four digits of the account in the respective blanks.)

The data reported about me is erroneous because (). (Insert your own reason or fill in the blank, as appropriate, with one of the following reasons: "This is not my account"; "I have never paid late"; "I paid this account in full"; "This account was included in my bankruptcy"; "The balance shown is incorrect"; or "This account was opened fraudulently, and I am the victim of identity theft.")

Indicated below are my full name, date of birth, Social Security number, and address for the past two years:

Full Name:
Date of Birth:
Social Security Number:
Address, City, State, Zip Code:

Also enclosed is a copy of () (Insert "my driver's license," "a recent utility bill," or "a recent credit-card statement.") so that you can verify my address and identity. Please investigate this matter promptly and delete the incorrect information as required by law.

Sincerely,

Your Signature
Your Name

Enclosures (List what you are enclosing. Only send copies, not originals. Also mention whether you are providing any supporting documents to prove your claim. By law this information must be forwarded by the credit bureau to the creditor, bill collector, or furnisher of the erroneous information.)

Author's Note

Thanks for reading my book. If you want to learn more about personal finance, investments, trading, and business, I suggest you follow my author page on Amazon. Through my books, I have decided to share with you the know-how that has allowed me to achieve my financial freedom, to accumulate wealth, and to live the life I want with my family.

My goal is to show you the path with useful and applicable information for reaching your targets. Only you will be able to tread that path as I did… and now, I'm sharing what I know.

To your wealth!

Dave R. W. Graham

©Copyright 2020 by Dave Robert Warren Graham

– All rights reserved –

Made in the USA
Middletown, DE
30 March 2021